# WRITING PICTURE BOOKS

## W

**WRITER'S DIGEST BOOKS**
Cincinnati, Ohio
www.writersdigest.com

ANN WHITFORD PAUL

# WRITING PICTURE BOOKS

A Hands-On Guide From
Story Creation to Publication

For more resources for writers, visit www.writersdigest.com/books.

To receive a free weekly e-mail newsletter delivering tips and updates about writing and about Writer's Digest products, register directly at http://newsletters.fw publications.com.

13  12  11  10  09     5  4  3  2  1

Distributed in Canada by Fraser Direct
100 Armstrong Avenue
Georgetown, Ontario, Canada  L7G 5S4
Tel: (905) 877-4411

Distributed in the U.K. and Europe by David & Charles
Brunel House, Newton Abbot, Devon, TQ12 4PU, England
Tel: (+44) 1626-323200, Fax: (+44) 1626-323319
E-mail: postmaster@davidandcharles.co.uk

Distributed in Australia by Capricorn Link
P.O. Box 704, Windsor, NSW 2756 Australia
Tel: (02) 4577-3555

Library of Congress Cataloging-in-Publication Data
Paul, Ann Whitford.
  Writing picture books : a hands-on guide from story creation to publication / Ann Whitford Paul. -- 1st ed.
      p. cm.
  ISBN 978-1-58297-556-6 (pbk. : alk. paper)
  1.  Picture books for children--Authorship. 2.  Children's literature--Marketing.
I. Title.
  PN147.5.P385 2009
  808.06'8--dc22                                                2009006088

Edited by Alice Pope
Designed by Terri Woesner
Production coordinated by Mark Griffin

# DEDICATION

This book is written in loving memory of Sue Alexander and is dedicated to anyone who has ever written or dreamed of writing a picture book.

A portion of the proceeds of this book will help fund the SCBWI (Society of Children's Book Writers and Illustrators) Barbara Karlin Runner-Up Grant to recognize and encourage the work of aspiring picture book writers.

# ABOUT THE AUTHOR

Ann Whitford Paul became inspired to write picture books after years of bedtime reading to her four children. She writes picture books, poetry and early readers. Her books have won numerous awards and recognition including a place on The New York Times Notable Books List, Carl Sandburg Award for Children's Literature, Bank Street College Best Books list, Notable Science and Social Studies Books, National Parenting Centers "Seal of Approval," and Recognition of Merit from the George C. Stone Center for Children's Books of the Claremont Graduate University, and they've been nominated for numerous state reading awards.

When not busy typing at her computer or teaching picture book writing at UCLA Extension, Ann can most often be found taking a long walk. Her hobbies include cooking, quilting, and knitting. She also loves to watch spiders spin their webs, snails paint their trails, and cats play with yarn.

She lives in Los Angeles and hopes you'll check out her Web site at www.annwhitfordpaul.net.

# TABLE OF CONTENTS

# PROLOGUE

*I love revisions. Where else in life can
spilled milk be transformed into ice cream?*
—*Katherine Patterson*


Completing a draft of your story is not the end of the writing process. It is only the beginning. Then you must shape your draft into a publishable manuscript. This is the fun part of writing. This is the time-consuming part of writing. This is what separates the amateur from the professional. *Writing Picture Books: A Hands-On Guide From Story Creation to Publication* will help you become a professional.

When I first put pen to paper, fingers to typewriter, I made all the mistakes editors lecture about at conferences. My stories were dotted with characters with cutesy names, like Sammy Skunk. I wrote about putting a child to bed from the mother's point of view. I inserted dull directions to the illustrator saying the character should be walking out the door or skipping down the walk. My characters were perfect children who never misbehaved, my plots were contrived with an adult conveniently turning up to solve the problem, and my language was duller than an engineering textbook.

But I thought my stories were so fabulous that an editor would call me with an offer as soon as she read them. When months later my stories finally returned with form rejection letters, I convinced myself these editors didn't know what they were missing.

After many form rejection letters (I'm a slow learner), it dawned on me—I had serious learning to do. So I signed up for classes, joined several different writing groups, attended conferences, and read every book I could find about writing.

The importance of revision (the process that takes place between the first draft and the final submission to an editor) slowly seeped into my brain. I wrote this book to help you and other writers understand this faster than I did.

Writers commonly have one of three reactions to their first drafts.

Here's one: Maybe you love your draft. I thought my story about Sammy Skunk saving his friends Billy Beaver, Suzy Squirrel, etc., from Coyote Carl's sharp teeth by spraying his horrible smell (big surprise there!) was imaginative, original, and word perfect. I sent it out immediately. Wrong!

Or you might have this second reaction: You become so enamored with writing you can't bear to change a word. You decide your story is hopeless and toss it into the trash.

I've done that, too. Once I wrote about a young Italian boy pulling up potatoes. Besides never having lived in Italy nor grown potatoes, the story felt thin ... so what if he struggles with those potatoes? Convinced my writing was terrible, I tore up my pages and moved on to something else.

Whether you love your words or hate them, some things in every first draft are worth saving and some things must be thrown away.

The third reaction, which we should all strive to have, is a combination of the first two. That's when a writer reads her first draft and decides it isn't bad. She knows it isn't good, either, so she's ready to play around with it and make it better. But what should she delete? What should she save?

That's the problem.

It's hard to be objective about what works and what doesn't in our stories. It's much easier for an outsider (forget your mom, your partner, or your adoring younger brother), who is not emotionally tied to you to determine that for you.

The key to improving your writing is to learn, as best as you can, how to be your own critic. You must develop ways to pull yourself back from your story and become an outside reader. How do you do that?

Many writers feel setting the manuscript aside for days, weeks, or months can break through the love-or-hate affair with one's writing. This can help, but few of us have the self-control to hide a story in a drawer or under a bed for the weeks, months, or years necessary to acquire that objectivity. There's no guarantee you'll have much of it even after all that time.

Other writers feel it's important to know the things they should look for in a revision—such as a strong opening, good plotting, and three-dimensional characters. Many books about writing for children list the areas to consider when going over a story. This can help, but it's still not enough. Knowing you should have a strong opening is useless unless you know the characteristics of a strong opening. While we strive to create well-rounded characters, few of us know how to recognize if our characters are flat or acting inconsistently.

Some writers don't even try to become their own critics. Instead they send off their manuscript to a friend or family member, or they take it to a writing group. Outside readers who understand the craft of writing for children can be helpful. But the process of taking one's story to outsiders can be time-consuming, especially as you redo your story and bring it back for more comments again and again. After too much of this back-and-forth, those outside readers who have seen your story over and over become attached to it and lose their objectivity. It becomes their story, too.

How much better for you to take responsibility for becoming your own best critic! You'd be able to bring a much-improved story to your outside critics and the back-and-forth process would be shortened.

This book offers a fresh way to gain outsider objectivity. Techniques discussed in the following chapters will help you turn into a dispassionate critic of your work and give you the skills to make the necessary changes to strengthen your writing. At the end of each chapter, exercises will help you see your story more clearly and suggest direction for your revision.

Note that revision is not a one-time thing. Every change will call for others. Stories rarely jump onto your computer screen in finished form. They evolve, and evolve, and evolve again. That's one of the pains, and one of the pleasures, of writing. Something as simple as substituting one word for another will have ramifications throughout the manuscript.

Over the years, I've found being playful while writing and revising makes my work more pleasant. Although this book discusses serious topics like character development, strong openings, the poetry of prose, endings, and much more, the revision techniques included here will take you back to your childhood. You'll use crayons, markers, scissors, and tape to help you shape your words into a salable story.

An added benefit will be a break from your computer. This book offers opportunities to stand up and stretch; to give your eyes, neck, and shoulders a rest from your seat and your screen. You'll use muscles that might have grown lazy.

Like my students at UCLA Extension and participants in my workshops, you'll cut, color, paste, and revise your way to publication. You can do it!

## WHAT'S NEXT?

Before we turn to specific revision techniques, put on your scholar's cap. It's impossible to write a picture book if you don't understand its form. That's what our first chapter is about.

Read on!

## BEFORE YOU GO ON

Activities in future chapters assume you have a story to revise. If you don't, now is the time to begin thinking about the picture book story you want to write. However, wait to write it until you read the following chapter.

4

BEFORE YOU WRITE YOUR STORY

# BECOMING A PICTURE BOOK SCHOLAR

 *Writing is a craft before it is an art.*
*—Donald M. Murray*

Having had your appendix out doesn't qualify you to perform an appendectomy, so why should having seen picture books as a child qualify you to write one?

You wouldn't start creating a software program without first reading up on computer theory, but some people think they can write a picture book without ever reading or studying contemporary picture books.

Picture books have a unique form and audience. In this chapter, you'll learn what a picture book is and how its audience impacts your writing. But first I'd like to tell you a true story.

Several years ago my family was enjoying a pleasant summer supper outside. We were talking about the state of education in the United States and the discussion grew loud and the feelings strong. With six eager participants, I tried, but couldn't get in a word. Frustrated at being so ignored, I pounded my fist on the table and shouted, "LISTEN TO ME! I HAVE SOMETHING TO SAY!"

My son Alan, sixteen years old at the time, looked at me incredulously. "Listen to you? Why should we listen to you? You write books for people who can't even read."

We all had a good laugh, and I'm happy to say they did let me speak my piece. Much later, mulling over his comment, I realized Alan had come up with the perfect start of the definition for a picture book.

## A PICTURE BOOK IS A BOOK FOR PEOPLE WHO CAN'T READ

Picture books are usually read by an adult reader to a nonreader. To that end, it combines words and pictures. The pictures are there to entice the nonreader to listen and also help construct meaning from the words. Picture books are traditionally directed toward young children. Today, some picture books and graphic novels are published for the fluent reader, but this book will focus on those books aimed at children ages two through eight.

Such picture books are divided into two categories: books aimed at the nonreader and picture storybooks written for either the emergent, or newly established, reader. Published picture books, whether hard- or softcover, are usually thirty-two pages long, but your manuscript, always double-spaced with one-inch borders all around, will consist of considerably fewer pages.

A Society of Children's Book Writers & Illustrators (SCBWI) survey found that picture book manuscripts range from one-half page up to as high as fifteen pages. Those at the top range would obviously be for independent readers.

The age of the audience and the length of their attention span determine the length of the manuscript. Most beginning writers overwrite. Every time I teach, at least one student hands in a 1,000-word manuscript for a two-year old. By the five-hundreth word, every two-year-old I know would be climbing off the reader's lap to stack blocks or set out cups for a tea party.

That's why manuscripts for children up to two years old (who are wiggly and have short attention spans) should be about one-half to one manuscript page. Usually these are published as board books. Pictures are the most important element in board books. There might be one sentence on a page ... sometimes just one word. Because the

pictures are critical to drawing the listener in, early board books are generally written and illustrated by the same person.

Children between the ages of two to five can sit still for more time, so their picture book manuscripts are longer—around two to five pages. With roughly 200 words per page, that means 400 to 900 words. When my manuscripts reach the 700-word range, or six pages, I get nervous and look for ways to cut.

Manuscripts between six pages and up to fifteen pages are for older children and adults. The longer the manuscript is, the more likely the book pages will increase ... always in multiples of eight. One book might be forty pages, another forty-eight, and so on. A word of caution: With each addition of eight pages, the book will cost more to produce.

If you've never been published, revise to fit your story into the thirty-two-page format. Publishers are wary of spending more money than necessary on an untried product.

Regardless of length, picture book writers must work hard to compel the reader to keep reading. Writers of longer works create end-of-chapter hooks so the reader won't put the book down. In picture books, we speak of these hooks as *page turns*. We motivate the reader to turn the page with an unanswered question, the placement of the main character in an uncomfortable situation, having the character take action so the outcome is in doubt, or simply a curiosity about what will happen next.

For an understanding of brilliant page turns, read *That's Good! That's Bad!* by Margery Cuyler. The story is written as a dialogue between the narrator and an invisible listener. In one section, the main character, a little boy, is in the jungle and wakens a snoring daddy lion. The listener says, "Oh, that's bad." The narrator answers, "No, that's good!" Most readers would think waking a sleeping lion is *very, very* bad. They would find it hard to believe an awake lion could ever be good. That's why they rush to turn the page where they discover that the lion purrs and even licks the boy's face. Throughout the story, whenever the listener says, "That's good" or "That's bad," the narrator contradicts. The reader and listener can hardly wait to find out why.

Because a picture book is both words and pictures, the writer can limit words to the bare essentials. In *The Best Place to Read* by Debbie Bertram and Susan Bloom, a little boy with a new book is searching for the best location to read his treasure. It's not in his chair he's outgrown. It's not in Grammy's cozy chair, because Rover loves it and won't move. It's especially not outside on a patio chair … when the sprinkler starts! Nowhere in the text do the authors describe their main character's clothes, the appearance of each different chair, or even the title of his new book. None of these are relevant to the forward momentum of the boy finding his perfect reading place. The writers wisely trusted the creativity of illustrator Michael Garland to handle the descriptions. You also don't need to describe the house the character lives in, the appearance of his parents, or the breed of his dog. Descriptions, *unless vital* to your story, should all be eliminated. That allows you, the writer, to focus on the **action** and **dialogue** of your story. Writers for the very young, even if they're not illustrators, still must have visual images in their minds. You want to write a text that allows the illustrator space for a variety of interesting picture possibilities to keep the listener involved with the book. You can do this in four ways:

1. Writing scenes with action.
2. Introducing new characters into the story.
3. Moving characters into different settings.
4. Changing the emotional intensity of a scene.

In picture books for two- to five-year-olds, the text requires pictures to tell the story. Writers should strive to leave room in their manuscripts for the illustrator to develop an independent picture story line. For a good example, read Laura Joffe Numeroff's *If You Give a Mouse a Cookie*. On one page in the story, Numeroff writes that the picture the mouse is drawing is done, but gives no indication of what the picture would look like. Instead she allows illustrator Felicia Bond to to create a fine artist-quality portrait of a mouse family in front of their tree-trunk house.

Sometimes not having all the details in the words allows the illustrator. In my book *If Animals Kissed Good Night* David Walker

depicts how a rabbit never mentioned in the text is shown frightened by a bear's growl. Also never mentioned in the text, but illustrated warmly, is a little girl in bed at the beginning and again near the end of the book. Good illustrators add their own story so the prereader can have fun "reading" the pictures. Good writers give the artists space to do that.

This is not true with a longer picture storybook. Here the words are more likely able to stand on their own. Although a storybook is fully illustrated, the pictures may show an aspect of the story but rarely add a new story line. The balance has been tipped from heavy with illustration to heavy with words. The writer has more room to expand the story and add details. Often, these books have large chunks of text that might even take up the entire page.

*Sweet Clara and the Freedom Quilt* by Deborah Hopkinson is over 2,000 words long and covers many years and numerous incidences in the life of a young slave girl who finally escapes to freedom. Some pages are text without illustration. The pictures by James Ransome echo the action but don't add a second story line as picture books for the younger child do.

This is true of many historical fiction picture books. *Sam and the Tigers* by Julius Lester and other original and retold tales can often be word heavy, too, as can books that deal with issues more appropriate for older children. *Old Turtle* by Douglas Wood, where the animals and people, and even clouds and breezes, contemplate God, is but one example.

We've considered the look and shape and size of a manuscript. It's time to consider the unusual two-part picture book audience.

## CHILDREN TWO TO EIGHT YEARS OLD

This is the targeted age for picture books. Bearing that in mind, it behooves all writers to get to know this audience and what matters to them. You will probably have difficulty writing for children if you don't have either a strong memory of your childhood or firsthand experience with those going through childhood. However, you can always educate yourself by spending time with nieces and nephews,

neighbors, etc. Here are some characteristics of children I try to keep in mind when I write.

## Everything Is New to Children

We adults have been in cars so often our minds sometimes travel elsewhere when we're behind the wheel. Yet children are fascinated by every tree, house, and shop they see from their backseat window. When my granddaughter Hazel was three years old, she loved long trips on the freeway so she could point out all the trucks that had *her* letter *H* on them.

A worm? We step right over it. A child squats down to watch it squirm. The world is a wonder to children, but most adults have grown blasé about it. As a children's writer, you must tap back into the excitement of new discovery. How?

Wonder happens automatically when you travel to a new place. But you don't have to fly to Africa to capture wonder—you can do it closer to home. Try something new. Visit a museum you've never been to before. Walk through an unfamiliar neighborhood. Try foods you think you don't like.

Be open to everything around you. In an unfamiliar store, notice the smells from the candy counter. Feel the smooth texture of a satin dress. Listen to the sounds the computer makes printing your receipt.

Don't be afraid to be foolish. Pretend to put yourself into a child's body; it's not as hard as it sounds. Make yourself small. Get down on your hands and knees. (I wouldn't recommend doing this at a store, however. Wait until you return home.) What do you notice at that lower level? Is the floor smooth? Hard? Cool? Does the cat look bigger to you from down there or smaller? Pick up a dust ball. Does it tickle?

Explore outside. Touch a snail's trail. Is it sticky? Chase a squirrel. Can you catch it? Dig in the dirt with your fingers. Is the dirt moist? Is it dry?

Then, when you are writing, put that wonder of the world in your words.

11

## Children Live in the Present

Anyone traveling with young children knows the question, "Are we there yet?"

You answer, "We'll be there in one hour."

Ten minutes later, they ask again. "Are we there yet?"

The concepts of *an hour from now*, *tomorrow*, or *next week* are not clear to young children. For that reason, picture books for this audience usually take place in a few hours, a day, or a night. Books that extend over a longer period of time are for older readers and often use a repetitive phrase to help anchor the listener. That phrase can be as mundane as "the next day" or as rooted to the story as "when I went to the beach with Grandpa."

## Children Have Had Few Experiences

That explains why they have a fit when a friend won't share blocks.

Or sob when their ice cream plops off the cone.

Or insist that only a hamburger will make them happy.

We adults have lived through many disappointments. We know there will be other times to share blocks, other chocolate cones to lick, and that, sometimes, chicken tastes better than hamburger.

Children don't know these things yet. They cry when left with a babysitter because they're worried their parents might not return—this is *their* high drama. As a writer, look for those seemingly small incidents that matter greatly to children.

In *Big Help!* by Anna Grossnickle Hines, a brother deals with his younger sister who wants to help but always gets in the way. In *Bunny Cakes* by Rosemary Wells, Max struggles to get the grocer to read his writing. These problems are not earth-shattering to adults, but they're vitally important to children.

## Children Have Strong Emotions

Anatole Broyard wrote, "When you're young, everything matters. Everything is serious."

If one's favorite shirt is in the laundry, an adult will shrug and put on another shirt. A child might throw a tantrum.

12

A child who doesn't want to go to bed may sob frantic tears. Being asked to give up one's special blanket is traumatic. If you want to see how upsetting this can be, read Kevin Henkes's Caldecott Honor Book, *Owen*. Children care deeply. Tap into their strong emotions for your stories.

## Sometimes Childhood Is Not Happy

Many of us look back on childhood as an idyllic time. Nothing to do but play with our favorite toys, eat food someone else cooked, and never have to work for a living.

What could be easier? What could be nicer? Children should appreciate how lucky they are not to have to pay bills, grocery shop, or drive in heavy traffic.

It's true that children don't have to do those things. But they do have to deal with bullies at school. They have to struggle to shape the letters of their name, and they're devastated if the friend they always sit next to at story time decides to sit next to someone else.

Tragic things happen to children. Pets die. Grandparents die. Parents die or leave to make another home. Read *I Remember Miss Perry* by Pat Brisson, which deals, with great sensitivity, with the sudden death of a beloved teacher.

Print yourself a sign that says CHILDHOOD IS NOT ALL SILLY AND JOYFUL. Post it near your computer. Remember it always. Remind yourself to think about the ups and the downs that happen to children.

Sometimes, because humor helps deal with problems, funny books can be beneficial in times of stress and worry. Judith Viorst, in her classic *The Tenth Good Thing About Barney*, uses humor to lighten the somber mood about the death of a cat. My favorite part is when the main character and narrator says one of the good things about Barney was that he ate a bird only one time. I can't help smiling every time I read that. Children also need books that deal in a thoughtful manner with the problems they face. For a poignant story about recovery from the death of a sibling, read Sue Alexander's haunting *Nadia the Willful*.

## Children Understand More Than We Think They Do

Sometimes they're smarter than adults. Certainly they are more intuitive. They trust their feelings and react to them. Children read, listen, and observe with their hearts.

Much as I tried to hide it, my children accurately sensed when, one year, I was angry with my husband for ignoring Mother's Day. They knew something was bothering me and became extra clingy.

Whenever I was in a hurry, my children understood, without my saying a word, and took extra long to find missing a shoe or make their lunches.

Writers don't need to explain too much. Children are wise enough to figure out what a story is about without tacking on a moral. We're in the business of writing engaging stories, not teaching lessons. Leave that to educators.

## Children Have Short Attention Spans

Unfortunately the intrusion of TV and video games doesn't encourage any lengthening of their attention spans. That's why we shouldn't write long and convoluted stories. Our stories must be focused—not about just one thing, but about one *aspect* of one thing.

Suppose you want to write about the ocean for a young audience. You will need to break down the subject like Tony Johnston did, looking at just whales in her book *Whale Song*. Also writing about the ocean, Alice Schertle focuses on a different aspect in *All You Need for a Beach*. And Eve Bunting in *Ducky* tells the tale of a rubber duck adrift in the ocean. Read these books to see how tightly focused each story is. There are unlimited ocean topics you, too, can write about—one special trip across the ocean, surfing, or a picnic by the ocean. One could spend a lifetime writing books for children about different aspects of the ocean.

Kurt Vonnegut Jr. said, "Don't put anything in a story that does not reveal character or advance the action." While he's talking about writing for adults, this advice is doubly important in picture books.

Every word, every sentence must be part of the whole and must lead to the ending.

## Children Are Self-Centered

We all are self-centered, but most adults hide it better. Children don't want to hear stories about teachers' or parents' problems. They want to hear stories about *their* problems. In this, they are not unlike adults. Surely, in your reading of adult fiction, you find some books more appealing than others. As a woman I'm more interested in those with a female character than a male character. If you're writing for children, make your characters children or childlike animals, like Russell Hoban did in *Bedtime for Frances*, or childlike adults as Kirby Larson did in *The Magic Kerchief*. Her main character is a white-haired woman named Griselda who can't stop herself from saying the truth no matter how it might upset people around her. Griselda was not much different than my little brother, who years ago peered under a woman's dress in the grocery checkout line. She was an amputee and he asked loudly, "Where is her other leg, Mommy?" Children don't yet know there are times when saying nothing is best.

## Children Long to Be Independent

Even though deep inside you know they are trying to be helpful, don't you hate it when someone tells you how to do something? Kids are that way, too. They want to do things themselves, and if we are good parents and educators, we give children the chance, in situations without danger, to try out and develop new skills. We encourage them to eat with a spoon, hold their own cups, or cut paper with blunt scissors.

And in our books we give them examples of strong girls and boys who find their own solutions to their problems. Our books should empower children, just like Jacqueline Woodson does in *The Other Side*. Here two young girls—one black and one white—without the help or interference of bigoted or fearful adults, forge a friendship together. In Karen Hesse's *The Cats in Krasinski Square*, the young girl

15

narrator comes up with the idea of how to stop the Gestapo and their dogs from sniffing out the people smuggling food into the ghetto.

## Children Are Complicated

They are like adults—not all good, and not all bad. Look for that gray area with your characters. Create well-rounded, not cookie-cutter, characters. (We'll discuss how to do this in chapter 6.) Hume Cronyn, the well-known actor, followed one rule in his work that easily applies to picture books: "If you're doing the devil, look for the angel in him. If you're doing the angel, look for the devil in him." This is another quotation you might want to put above your computer.

In the charming Rotten Ralph books by Jack Gantos we realize, along with Sarah, that her cat Ralph is not *always* rotten. Sometimes he does try to do the right thing.

## Children Have Rich Imaginations

Because they lack experience in the world, they are able to accept the possibility of many things that adults know are impossible. A little boy can be carried by a balloon around the world. A frog and a toad can speak. Animals at the zoo can read books. Children's imaginations soar. Let your imagination soar with them.

So far we've focused on the child audience, but since these children are too young to read and too young to pay for a picture book, we must consider our other audience.

## ADULT AUDIENCE

These are parents, grandparents, teachers, and librarians. who read out loud to children. This double audience puts picture books in a class by themselves and has great ramifications for your writing.

## Language Does Not Have to Be Babyish

Because you want to appeal to the adult reader, you should not feel constrained to use only simple, childlike language. Words like

*itty-bitty* and *dimple dumpling* are trite, overused, and demeaning in picture books.

Don't tie yourself to age-level word lists, either. Part of your job as a writer is to introduce children to the pleasures of our language. Feel free to use big and unusual words *if* their meaning is clear in the context of your story and *if* they're not too difficult to read out loud.

The word *discrimination*, which a picture book aged child might not understand, can still be used in a story if you write something like: Jesse's grandfather faced much discrimination when he was growing up. *He couldn't swim in the town's pool. He had to ride in the back of the bus. And some restaurants refused to serve him … all because his skin was dark.*

By giving specific examples, we help the child see what *discrimination* means and also increase her vocabulary.

## Make Books Easy to Read Out Loud

Think about the adults reading your books. While one of them might be Julia Roberts, most likely your readers will be ordinary people who aren't professional actors.

Your words must give plenty of opportunity for the nontheatrically trained adult to sound like he graduated from the Yale School of Drama. How do you do that?

Besides avoiding words adults have difficulty pronouncing, don't write humongous sentences like this one that will make your poor unsuspecting reader gasp for breath way before reaching the desperately needed punctuation mark that finally at long last signifies the end.

Dialogue helps your reader. It's easier to put expression into what characters are saying than in sections of narrative description.

Onomatopoetic words like *BOOM, CRASH,* and *BUZZ* are always amusing and invite the young prereader to join in.

But the best help you can give your reader is to understand poetry and use its techniques in your writing.

"Help!" I hear you moaning. "I hate poetry. If I have to write poetry, I'll never do a picture book."

17

Take a deep breath, close your eyes, and tell yourself, "Poetry is my friend." Anyone with the drive and willingness to put in the necessary hard work can learn the craft of writing picture books. This includes poetry. So read each chapter and do the exercises in the order written. Eventually you will get to later chapters on rhythm and word sounds, and I guarantee you will enjoy making your stories more poetic.

## Adults Are Frequently Asked to Read Picture Books Again ...

... and again. Have compassion for your adult reader. Picture books are short not only for the child, but also for the adult. My children often asked me to read their favorite books two, three, even four times. How grateful I was for brevity! Who wants to read a 3,000-word book over and over again in one sitting? Not me!

Also, picture books are getting more expensive every day. Adults want their money's worth from our short stories. That's why you need to give adult readers and their young listeners a story that will stay with them. Your writing must strike an emotional chord in each one and bring them eagerly back to your book time and again.

After each chapter, one of the assignments will be to read a picture book that is new to you. One book after each chapter means you'll have read twenty by this book's end, and you'll be well on your way to becoming an expert. The more you read, and the more you think about what you read, the faster you'll reach that goal of publication.

---

WHAT'S NEXT?

---

In chapter 2, we're going to learn how to write a story that will appeal to both adults and children and make them want to read and hear your story over and over.

---

## BEFORE YOU GO ON

1. Spend time reading picture books. It would be especially helpful if you looked at some of the books mentioned in this and future chapters. But don't just read them—think about them. Take notes. Study why one works for you and another doesn't. This is good training before starting to write and should continue throughout your career.

2. Choose a published picture book you love. Choose one you think is so dreadful it never should have been published.

"Wait a minute," you say. "Why would anyone publish an awful book?"

Publishing houses don't intend to publish bad books. Someone working there loved the manuscript. Someone saw a market for the book.

How many times has a friend raved about a book and you rushed out to buy it, only to discover you hated it? Choosing which books to publish depends on an editor's taste, which may not coincide with yours.

On the other hand, it's also true that sometimes mistakes are made. We all make mistakes. That's part of the human condition. Accept it. Then you won't be so hard on yourself, or on others, when wrong choices are made. Now is as good a time as any to push away those thoughts that publishers and editors are infallible. Don't give them so much power. They are human beings with strengths and weaknesses, likes and dislikes, just as we all are.

Make sure each of the books has been published within the last five years. Styles change in books as fast as they change in fashion. Books published in the 1960s are far different from books being published in the twenty-first century.

Type the good and bad manuscripts into your computer so you can print them out easily. Take a closer look at these picture books. Using what you have just learned about the form of a picture book and the different audiences of picture books, take notes on why they do or don't work. (A writing friend critiquing this manuscript said that instead of just one good and bad picture book, I should have you read piles of each kind of book. Her advice is good. You will improve your writing immeasurably by reading many picture books, but I don't want to overwhelm you with work. So for the purposes of this book, one good and one bad book will suffice.)

"Why waste my time doing this?" you ask. "Why not just work on my own book?"

First of all, you'll discover why one book works and the other doesn't. More importantly, you'll have two manuscripts to compare to your own. In most of the chapters, you will be asked to do exercises on your story. I encourage you also to do these on the manuscripts you typed into your computer. If you have any questions about the concepts in this book, exploring them on your already published books will help clarify the issues. If you're fortunate enough to already belong to a writing group—we'll explore how to create and run one in chapter 18—you might do these exercises on published books with your members.

3. Read a new picture book.

4. Ta-da! Time to write! You know what a picture book is. You've read some picture books. You've typed up a good picture book and a bad picture book. If you haven't done so already, write your story. Relax. Have fun with this. Remember, your first draft will rarely be ready to submit to an editor. Just as milk needs churning to become ice cream, your draft will need revision to become publishable. Get your story down and you'll have something to work with.

EARLY STORY DECISIONS

# BUILDING A FRAME FOR YOUR STORY HOUSE

 *The story must be short, but the idea tall enough to be made into a book.* —*Lee Wyndham*

We've just finished talking about the unusual quality of picture books having two audiences: adults (parents, grandparents, teachers, librarians, who pay the money for the book) and the children who listen to the adult reader.

Hopefully the stories we write will appeal to both of them so they will want to share the book together more than once. Better yet, the children will love the book so much that when they reach adulthood they will want to read it to their children. This is how classics like *The Story of Ferdinand* by Munro Leaf, *Where the Wild Things Are* by Maurice Sendak, and *Bedtime for Frances* by Russell Hoban are born.

Too often, however, picture book stories appeal to one audience only. As a parent, many books my children loved, I couldn't abide. I'm sorry to say I often stooped to immature behavior, hiding an offensive book under a bed or tucking it behind other books on the shelf. Sometimes it mysteriously disappeared forever.

Then there were the books that appealed to me but not to my children. Because I had control (which comes from being the grown-up reader), they had to accede to my wishes. I knew which books these were because my children never chose to share them. Instead I would foist them on their unwilling ears. They only tolerated this because the bargain was that afterwards I would read one of their favorites. And what child doesn't want to sit a bit longer in an adult's arms listening to a story, even one he doesn't like, when there's another, better one waiting to be heard?

Obviously the ideal picture book must appeal to both adults and children. The best way to ensure this is to make sure your story depth resonates with both the reader and the listener.

What makes a story have such depth?

Enduring picture books must be about something bigger than a mere incident. The story problem must explore some large theme or issue. It must have a kernel of truth about life and our world.

Writing about a little girl's walk and the pebble she puts in her pocket, the dog that barks at her, and the neighbor who waves a greeting has no larger truth. It's merely an incident, a vignette, a description. The writer must have an idea, or theme, in the back of her mind that she's investigating. She must have something that will turn such a set of incidents into a story that stays with the reader long after the book is closed.

The process of building a story is like building a house. A carpenter cannot put up the walls until he builds a frame. The frame holds up the walls. The frame supports the roof. The frame determines the final shape of the house.

Your story frame determines everything—plot, characters, ending, word usage. To discover your story frame, you don't need a hammer or a saw. You don't need tools or expensive gadgets. There's only one thing you require, and it's free.

## STORY QUESTION

It behooves writers to think of a general question about the underlying issue they are trying to unravel in each new story.

Remember that little girl's walk around the block? Let's add something to it for the writer to investigate. Suppose the little girl is walking to her grandmother's house at the end of the block and she is supposed to get there in ten minutes. She pauses not only to pick up a pebble, but also to smell a flower and to trace a snail's trail.

Each of those pauses takes on more importance because she must arrive at her grandmother's within a certain time period. Perhaps the story question now might be: *What happens when we pay attention to the everyday wonders of nature?*

To better understand this concept, let's look at the story questions in some well-known published books.

In the popular *The Story of Ferdinand* by Munro Leaf, the general question might be: *What occurs when someone, or some animal, is forced to behave in a way not true to his character?*

In the successful book *Click, Clack, Moo: Cows That Type* by Doreen Cronin, the general question is: *How do we bring about change?*

In Melinda Long's delightful *How I Became a Pirate*, the question might be: *What would we discover if we had an opportunity to become something we'd always fantasized about?*

Of course there are many different ways the story question can be asked—as many ways as the number of people asking it. Another person might word the question in *How I Became a Pirate*: *What happens when someone goes to an exotic place?* Another person might put the story question this way: *Where is the best place to be?* These questions all approach the same general issue. Not everyone has to agree on the exact wording of the question, but **it is critical each story has a question** and that, no matter how worded, the intent of the inquiry is the same. If it is not, the story probably is not focused.

In addition, notice that I said "a" question. Picture books are brief, and your child audience's attention span is too short to explore more than one question at a time. Knowing your story question is crucial in keeping your writing tight and focused. Your question lays a set of tracks that keep a train traveling to its destination. Too often writers start out exploring one question and then switch tracks to explore another. Discovering your question will keep your story moving in the right direction.

You may worry that asking a question might lead to a preachy and didactic story. Just remember that the question you are exploring is never written into your text. It only needs to be bold and strong in *your* mind. Let your story evolve, and trust that the question will be understood on *some* level by your readers and listeners.

Do you need to know your story question before you start writing? For some writers, the answer is yes. They cannot begin unless they have an idea of what they want to say.

But for many others, writing is a matter of discovery. Sometimes the story question may not be obvious in the beginning.

That's fine.

But the important thing is that sooner or later you must find, and be able to state concisely, this question. Otherwise your writing runs the risk of meandering.

## STORY ANSWER

Let's assume you know the question you are exploring. Then it's time to answer your question in a manner specific to your story. One sentence should be all it takes.

Let's go back to the little girl walking around the block. The question proposed was: What happens when we pay attention to the everyday wonders of nature?

The answer might be: A young girl is so entranced by the pebbles, flowers, and a snail that, in spite of her good intentions to hurry to her grandmother's, she cannot help but stop and admire nature's work.

What about those published books we asked questions for? What might their answers be?

The question in *The Story of Ferdinand* was: What occurs when someone is forced to behave in a way not true to that character?

My answer would be: Ferdinand, when compelled to participate in the bullfights, flatly refuses and finally is returned home, where he is allowed to sit and smell the flowers and be himself.

In *Click, Clack, Moo: Cows That Type*, the question was: How do we bring about change?

The answer might be: Farmer Brown's cows, unhappy with the conditions in their barn, go on strike and, joined by the hens and aided by the ducks, force Farmer Brown to accede to their demands.

In *How I Became a Pirate* the question was: What would we discover if we had an opportunity to become something we'd always fantasized about?

The answer might be: A young boy gets a chance to follow his dream of being a pirate but learns seafaring life is not all it's cracked up to be.

Notice that the answer is a short blurb about the book. In the movie business, this is called a *pitch*. If you cannot answer *in one sentence* what happens in your story, you may have a problem with too much going on. Spend time carefully formulating your question and answer. If you do, the writing of your book will be infinitely easier.

## QUESTION AND ANSWER IN CONCEPT BOOKS

Some writing for children does not tell a story. It explores a subject like shadows, hands, or water. We call these *concept books*. Does the story question-and-answer principle still apply?

Absolutely, but in such cases the question is expressed more specifically to the book.

Let's look at Ruth Krauss's classic *A Hole Is to Dig*. The story question here might be: Would children's definitions of everyday objects be different from a normal dictionary?

And the answer would be: Yes. Their definitions often have to do with the function of an object as it relates to them.

In a more contemporary book, *All You Need for a Snowman* by Alice Schertle, the question would be: *What do you need to make a snowman?*

The answer would also be story specific: To build a snowman you need lots of snow and clothes and things for the eyes and nose and mouth, and last of all, another snow friend.

Vicki Cobb, in her book *I See Myself*, asks: *How do we see ourselves in a mirror?*

Her answer is: To see ourselves in a mirror we need light and the smooth surface of the glass.

Whether you are writing a story or merely exploring a concept, it's not enough to just know your question and answer. You need to keep it in mind through all your revisions. Follow your story road map. Make sure you don't drive to New York when you want to go to Florida. Don't lose your way. Otherwise you might start out writing a story about a boy who wants his big brother to play more with him, but veer off into a new problem of convincing his mother he's old enough to go to the drugstore by himself.

When I'm working on a story, I keep my question and answer in my computer to refer to constantly. You might prefer to tack it on a bulletin board or use a sticky note to stick on your computer. Whatever you do, make sure once you have determined it, you stick to it. Go through your story line by line and delete anything that doesn't have to do with the story question and answer. Remember how short and focused picture books must be. Your question and answer will keep you on the right track.

For example, in my book *If Animals Kissed Good Night,* my question was: If animals kissed good night, how might they do it? Keeping this firmly in mind kept me from writing about how animals gathered food, who their predators were, or where they lived. All of those subjects, albeit interesting, had nothing to do with my question and therefore didn't belong in my story.

## MULTIPLE LEVELS IN A BOOK

One other way to appeal to both your adult and child audience is to make sure your book has multiple levels. Books that are loved by parents and children, and that can be employed by teachers to illustrate concepts in their curriculum, will obviously increase sales.

Years ago, a random listing of objects was enough for an alphabet book. Then publishing houses wanted alphabet books around a theme such as animals or flowers. Now alphabet books have to do more. They also have to tell a story. Look at my book *Everything to Spend the Night*, where a little girl packs her suitcase for a sleepover at Grandpa's with everything from *A* to *Z*. Unfortunately she forgets her most important thing—pajamas. In June Sobel's *B Is for Bulldozer: A Construction ABC*, the builders are creating a roller coaster. In both of these books, while learning one's ABCs, the listener is also hearing a story. That's what I mean by more than one level.

The apparently simple *Diary of a Wombat* by Jackie French actually has three levels. First, it's a charming story about the conflict of a wombat with his new human neighbors. Second, it gives information about wombats. Third, it follows the days of the week, a feature that a teacher might find useful in his classroom.

*The Other Side* by Jacqueline Woodson tells about the friendship between two children of different races. Besides being able to stand on its own, this book provides teachers with a poignant story to share with students each year around Martin Luther King Jr.'s birthday.

*The Alphabet Atlas* by Arthur Yorinks is an alphabet book that also introduces readers to the countries of the world. Additionally the art introduces children to the craft of quilting, perhaps inspiring them and their adult readers to try their own stitching.

Obviously a writer shouldn't add extra levels merely to be adding them. My point is that a story with more than one level has a better chance of longer shelf life, certainly in schools and libraries, than one that does not. And isn't a long life what we want for all of our books?

## WHAT'S NEXT?

Now that we've discussed how important it is to have something to say in your story, we're moving on to chapter 3, the first of three chapters on determining the best way to tell your story.

## BEFORE YOU GO ON

1. Write a story question and answer for the story you wrote. Do you have a friend or fellow writer you could share your story with? Ask her to write what she thinks is the story question and answer. If your friend's question is wildly different than yours, you know your writing is not clear, or perhaps you are exploring something other than what you think. Either one will force you to consider revisions. Once your question and answer are determined to your satisfaction, go through your story and highlight anything that does not bear directly on them. Then delete. And revise.

2. Write the story question and answer for both your good and bad published books.

Then, using a pen, cross off anything that does not relate to that question and answer. Perhaps the reason your book is bad is that it doesn't answer any general question. Its problem may be that it's unfocused.

3. Read a new picture book.

# TELLING YOUR STORY
# —PART ONE

*The work of art as completely realized is
the result of a long and complex process
of exploration.* —Joyce Cary

Remember when you were young, how you loved dressing up like
Little Red Riding Hood or Superman? Remember how you changed
clothes, depending on what games you were playing? Maybe you put
on a fireman's hat. Maybe you wore a crown.

What, you ask, does playing dress-up have to do with writing
picture books? A lot!

In the same way you changed outfits, you can change your story
by telling it in different ways—so many possible ways that I've divided
them into three parts. This first section covers point of view, or POV.

Most picture book stories are told by an *outside* narrator who
speaks of the characters using the third-person pronouns *he, she, it,*
or *they*. In a completely unscientific study of thirty picture books
picked from my bookshelf, the vast majority, twenty-six total, were
written in the third person.

Only three of the stories were told by a character that was a *participant* in the story or a first-person narrator.

That adds up to a total of twenty-nine.

And the one odd-duck story?

That was Robert Kraus's *Whose Mouse Are You?*, told in the form of a conversation between an outside observer and a mouse.

In my classes and workshops, I always go around the room asking each student to read the first paragraph of his or her story. The results are consistent with my bookshelf experience.

Test it for yourself with picture books on your shelves or in the library. You, too, will find that the vast majority of books will be told in the manner of an outside narrator, or the third person.

The novelist Willa Cather said, "There are only two or three human stories, and they go on repeating themselves as fiercely as if they had never happened before." If we accept her statement as fact, the only way we can differentiate our writing from the other stories on the same topic is to write them uniquely. You want to make your story so original that it will leap into the hands of an editor and shout, "Publish ME!"

To do that, experiment and explore different ways to tell your story. Try something new and open up your story in amazing ways.

Let's play around with a familiar story from 600 B.C.

### The Goose With the Golden Eggs
By Aesop

A farmer went to the nest of his goose to see whether she had laid an egg. To his surprise he found, instead of an ordinary goose egg, an egg of solid gold. Seizing the golden egg he rushed to the house in great excitement to show it to his wife.

Every day thereafter the goose laid an egg of pure gold. But as the farmer grew rich, he grew greedy. And thinking that if he killed the goose he could have all her treasure at once, he cut her open only to find—nothing at all.

Application: The greedy who want more lose all.

# NARRATIVE VOICE—
# THIRD PERSON, SINGLE POV

The story above is told in the traditional and popular form of an outside observer who does not participate in the action but relates what happened in the story. Notice that the narrator doesn't go into the

goose's head. He stays with just one character—the farmer. As you've seen from my informal study and yours, too, most picture books are told in this manner of a single outside observer who usually goes into the head of only the main character.

*Little Mouse's Big Valentine* by Thacher Hurd tells the story of Little Mouse, who has made a big valentine, but all his friends turn it down because it's too bright, too big, or too silly. We only know what the other characters think by what they say. The narrator does not allow us into their heads. Little Mouse is on stage each page. He's never out of our sight.

## CHANGE THE POV CHARACTER

What happens if I tell this story with the goose as our main character?

> Goose sat in her nest waiting for Farmer Jones to come and take her egg.
> Just like clockwork, he arrived as the sun was rising.
> Goose watched him turn her egg over and over in his hands. Had she laid a rotten egg? Impossible!
> But something was different with her egg.
> Goose couldn't imagine what.

This offers a fun alternative on the usual tale. Of course, it will force the writer to change not only the ending, but much of the middle as well. A children's story probably can't be told from the POV of a character who is hacked to death. (Although the more I write, and read, the more I realize *nothing* is impossible.) Notice this example is still told from only one POV—the goose's.

A book that turns the tables on a classic story is *The True Story of the 3 Little Pigs! by A. Wolf* by Jon Scieszka. Instead of the traditional manner of telling the story from the pigs' POV, this version is told from the wolf's, with hilarious results.

## THIRD-PERSON OMNISCIENT (OR MULTIPLE) POV

Let's see how the golden egg story might read if the narrator jumps back and forth and in and out of the heads of each different character.

A farmer went to his goose's nest to see whether she had laid an egg.

Goose looked up at him with alarm. She flapped and honked and tried everything in her power to send him away.

But the farmer wanted an egg for breakfast. He wouldn't give up. After a long back-and-forth, he finally snatched the egg away. He studied it for a long time.

Goose watched him rush to the house. She had an uneasy feeling that trouble was fast approaching.

While older readers can move from one character's POV to another's easily, picture book listeners have more trouble. Why?

Remember, our young audience is new to books. It's best to make it as easy as possible for them to follow the action. Staying in one character's mind allows the listener to know whom to focus on and identify with. However, that said, *Big Pumpkin* by Erica Silverman is an example of a successful book told in the third-person omniscient POV. The story starts in the witch's mind when we learn she wants to bake a pumpkin pie. Later the narrator moves into the the ghost's and the vampire's minds as well to let readers know they longed for some of that pie, too. In a single POV narration the story would be told only from the witch's POV, and we would never know what the other characters are thinking.

# FIRST-PERSON STORY, OR TOLD IN THE LYRICAL VOICE

In this voice, the narrator becomes a participant in the story. Key words to let you know you're in a first person story are *I* and *we*. This voice allows you to deal more immediately and in more detail with feelings and internal thinking. If I'm having trouble getting into my character's head, I may write a version in this voice to get to know her better. Perhaps I'll like it and leave it in the lyrical voice, but I may rewrite it again in third person. The experimentation wasn't wasted, though, because I gained a deeper understanding of my character's feelings.

However, this voice also has some drawbacks. Telling your story in first-person doesn't allow you an opportunity to write about actions happening offstage. The main character, the I-writer, must be on every page. Also, telling it in this manner might give away the ending. At the very least, the reader will know the narrator survived to the end of the story. We might not know in what state he survived, but we are certain he lived long enough to tell the tale.

What happens when I change the beginning of *The Goose With the Golden Eggs* into the first-person voice of the farmer?

> One day I went to my goose's nest to see if she had laid an egg.
>
> I couldn't believe what was there—an egg, yes, the same size of any goose egg, but this egg was different.
>
> It was made of gold!
>
> It glittered and gleamed! I blinked in the brightness.

With this first-person voice, listeners experience the action and emotion along with the farmer. They get into his head and feel his wonder of that miraculous egg. Notice how the tone of the story has changed.

*The Wednesday Surprise* by Eve Bunting is narrated by a young girl, Anna, whom we are with throughout the story. We see what she wants us to see and feel her increasing excitement when she says things, like "My heart's beating awfully fast" and "I hold it [a rock], imagining I can still feel the desert sun hot inside it."

Note that you can also change your story, as we did, in the narrative voice by switching the POV character. I'm going to tell the story now, in the first person, but this time Goose will tell the story.

> I knew something was different with this egg, because I've never had so much trouble pushing one out. And no wonder! The egg was very heavy. And solid gold!

You can see how if you wrote this story to the end, it would definitely not be the story we started out with. That change is what we're after—something to liven up a tired and many-times-told tale.

First-person voices can also be written in different forms.

## One Long Letter

Dear Wife,

I'm so glad your mother is improving.

Although I miss you, life has been good here—amazingly good.

You won't believe what happened. Goose laid a golden egg. Yes, a solid gold egg! I immediately rushed to town and deposited it in the bank. Day after day she kept laying those eggs. We're rich.

But, knowing how much you love fine things, I decided to get all the treasure inside Goose. Using my hatchet, I made quick work of her.

What a stupid fellow I was! No golden eggs did I find. And now Goose is dead.

Please don't be angry.

My favorite example of a published book told in a single-letter form is Ann Turner's *Nettie's Trip South*. In this compelling story, Nettie writes to her friend Addie about her experiences visiting the south just before the civil war. One incident she describes is attending a slave auction and the horror of watching two young children being separated. She returns home forever changed.

## Journal or Diary

**Monday**

Dear Diary,

Thank heavens I have a place to share things I cannot share with my wife. If she finds out what has happened she'll only want more and more.

This morning my goose laid a golden egg. Solid gold! I hid it in the barn.

I pray what happened this morning is a fluke, and tomorrow Goose will lay a normal egg.

**Tuesday**

Dear Diary,

Oh, no! Today there was another solid gold egg.

And on and on with more entries ...

*Diary of a Wombat* by Jackie French is written as a journal. Wombat relates snippets of his life in a straightforward, no-nonsense voice. He includes many entries that say just one or two of the same words over and over again. *Slept. Ate grass. Scratched.* But in between that sleeping and eating and scratching, some new neighbors moved in and problems quickly ensued.

But now it's time to be a bit more daring with the story.

## SECOND PERSON

The word *you* is a clue here. Using *you*, the author turns the reader into a character in the story. I'm going to tell Aesop's fable in this voice. See how it plays out.

> You wake up one morning, thinking this will be like ever other day. You take a quick shower, put on your work clothes, and set out on your first chore of the day—collecting eggs from your goose.

*Written Anything Good Lately?* by Susan Allen and Jane Lindaman is an alphabet book about different forms of writing—autobiography, book report, and so on—but in the first sentence, which is the same as the title, "Written anything good lately?," they address the listener. The last sentence again speaks to that listener: "What have **you** written lately?"

Notice in all the examples above, I did not switch the narrator or the voice midstory. This would obviously confuse our younger audience. They wouldn't know who the main character was any more or with whom to identify. Once you start a picture book in one manner, stick to it.

Okay. You've read some ways you can change how you tell your story. Let's make sure you recognize the voices we've covered here—third-person narrative POV, first-person lyrical voice, one long letter format, second-person POV, and diary format or journal. On a separate piece of paper, write the names of the voices you think match these examples.

1. Columbus was an explorer.

2. February 1. We celebrated my birthday today.
   February 2. Seven years feels really old.

3. You want to be big. You want to be really big. You want
   to be so big you can beat up anyone—even the bully up
   ahead waiting to torment you.

4. I hate surprises.

5. Jimmy wishes his friend Billy would go away. Billy wonders why Jimmy doesn't want to play.

6. Dear George,
   I thought I loved you, but I don't. I love Jon instead.

7. Have you ever imagined what a dog dreams about?

8. Dear Diary, I'll remember this day as long as I live.

9. On my first day of school, I tripped over a log and broke
   my leg. Now I have to sit inside each recess and help the
   teacher. Bummer!

10. Jimmy ran into the house, slammed down his books and
    shouted, "Dad!"

11. Sue hates math. Becky hates spelling. Alan hates math,
    spelling, and reading, too.

Now let's see how well you did.

1. Third-person narrative POV. 2. First-person diary format.
3. Second-person POV. 4. First-person lyrical voice. 5. Third-person
multiple POV. 6. One long letter format. 7. Second-person POV.
8. Diary format or journal. 9. First-person lyrical voice. 10. Third-
person narrative POV. 11. Third-person multiple POV.

## WHAT'S NEXT?

We've tried several fairly basic writing voices here. It's time to go wild. In chapter 4, we're going to consider more unusual and dramatic ways to write your story.

## BEFORE YOU GO ON

1. Rewrite the opening paragraph in your story in at least three of these different forms. If you have time, do all of them.

   a. Third-person narrative voice—single POV
   b. Change your POV character
   c. Narrative voice—multiple POV
   d. First-person lyrical voice
   e. First-person lyrical voice, change your POV character
   f. First-person lyrical voice—one long letter
   g. First-person lyrical voice—diary or journal
   h. Second person

While you're writing these different opening paragraphs, be playful. Let your imagination run wild. See how your experiments will take your story in new and surprising directions.

2. Do you like one of these new voices? Write your story through to the end in it. But if you're not thrilled with any of these, don't be discouraged. Turn the page and see how else you can approach telling your story.

3. Read a new picture book.

# 4

# TELLING YOUR STORY —PART TWO

*In baseball you only get three swings
and you're out. In rewriting, you get almost as many
swings as you want and you know, sooner or later,
you'll hit the ball.* —Neil Simon

We've covered some basic ways to tell a story in the last chapter, and you've experimented with a few of them in your manuscript. Maybe you liked one and continued to write the story in that voice.

Good.

But maybe nothing seemed to improve your story or take it in a direction you felt comfortable with.

Don't give up.

As Neil Simon describes above, writers get as many swings as they want, or need, to get a hit book.

We're going to look at some outrageous ways to change your story and make it more enticing to that hard-to-please editor just waiting to reject manuscripts. In this chapter, we're going to cover three dramatic voices.

## APOSTROPHE VOICE

In this voice, the writer speaks to something in the story that can't speak back. From personal experience, I can attest to how this can

give new life to a story. In my book *Hello Toes! Hello Feet!*, the first several (okay, I admit it, many) versions were told with the narrative voice. It opened like this:

> These are Jon's toes.
> These are Jon's feet,
> tangled up between his sheets.
> First his feet touch the floor.
> They hop him to the closet door.

And on ... and on ... and on ...

The manuscript was finished, I thought, but I took it back to my writing group because I had a niggling feeling that the story fell flat. I expressed my misgivings and someone suggested I experiment and have the main character (who at the time was my son Jon) talk to his feet. A lightbulb switched on in my head.

I rushed home to my computer and changed the opening to this:

> Good morning, toes,
> Good morning, feet,
> tangled up between
> my sheets.
> Be the first to touch the floor,
> hop me to the closet door.

Then I wrote in that voice all the way to the end. It worked! The manuscript suddenly became alive and vibrant to me. And my editor agreed.

The one thing she and I differed on was that the character wasn't a little boy like my son Jon. The illustrator, Nadine Bernard Westcott, agreed with my editor and made her a spunky little girl with blond hair and a green ribbon in her hair. That's the joy of collaboration. Other people take your words and go with them in new directions. Although I was sad to leave Jon behind, I'm thrilled with how the book came out. And eventually, inspired by my son who rarely puts anything off, I created Iguana in *Mañana, Iguana*. I finally used Jon as a character. That's why the book is dedicated to him.

Experimenting with speaking to different characters and things can make a dull story shine.

Let's go back and see what would happen in Aesop's *The Goose With the Golden Eggs* if the narrator spoke to the goose. It might go something like this:

> Goose, you sure are guarding that egg closely.
> Come on! Get up!
> MOVE!

Look at *Sit, Truman!* by Dan Harper, where the narrator speaks to Truman, a very big dog with a mind of his own.

A word of warning: I've not seen a successful attempt of using the apostrophe voice talking to more than one character, probably because it might be confusing for the young listener. It's best to keep this voice simple, and talk to the same character or object throughout.

# MASK VOICE

In this voice, the narrator becomes an inanimate object like a tree, a desk, or a bed and tells the story through that object's POV. This voice allows the imagination to run wild. No one, for example, knows how a tree feels when it rains, so I can play it for all it's worth. Let's try this voice with our Aesop fable:

> When I first came into this world, I found myself lying on something scratchy and uncomfortable. I learned later it was hay. I could hardly breathe because something soft and warm enclosed me. Imagine how happy I was when my mother climbed off of me.

Several problems make using this voice tricky. The first is how will the egg be illustrated? Will it have a mouth and eyes and ears? The pictures have a danger of bordering on the cute side, which we want to avoid. This a risk even if you tell your story as Watty Piper did in *The Little Engine That Could,* by an outside observer who is able to get into the inanimate object's mind. When Piper described the train as happy, the illustrators of the 1954 edition, George and Doris Hauman, showed this by putting a smiley face on the engine.

Another problem is that many inanimate objects, such as a tree, a skyscraper or a brige, stay stuck in place forever. Because they can't be moved, they can't talk about anything that takes place out of their view, leading to possibly static illustrations that don't change scene. A tree would be stuck in one place. However, in our example, the pictures might not be so repetitive because an egg can be moved. But the egg can't ever know what is happening outside of its immediate vision or hearing (assuming that the inanimate egg object has ears and eyes!).

But when it's done successfully, as Eve Bunting does in *I Am the Mummy Heb-Nefert*, this manner of telling is definitely dramatic.

> I am the mummy Heb-Nefert,
> black as night,
> stretched as tight
> as leather on a drum.

After this opening, the mummy tells about her life on earth—how she danced and sailed and lived and loved. While this might seem an obvious use of the mask voice, because the character was once alive, look at *Heartland* by Diane Siebert for a completely different sense of technique. The narrator is the heartland and speaks, always in the first person *I*, of rivers and cities and farms, of cornfields and seasons and the different lives people pursue there. Note that because the narrator, the whole middle of America, is so grand, the pictures can be varied.

Trying out new voices on your story is never a waste of time. Any experimentation you do will enrich your vision of it. You are forced to think outside the box, and that is what can make your story different and distinctive and salable.

# CONVERSATION VOICE

This voice is just what it says: a conversation between two characters. Nothing more. No narrative description. No *he said, she said,* or *it said.* It can be between two persons or two animals (assuming they can talk) or between a person and an animal, as long as you write nothing but the words they say.

Let's pretend our farmer and the goose can speak to one another.

> Goose! What's up with you? Why are you hiding your egg from me?
> *Because you always take my eggs away. Let me keep this one … please!*
> You want to keep one? That must be a special egg. Let me have a look and then I'll let you keep it.
> *No you won't! You'll take it away from me. I know.*

I can't repeat enough that you will find no narrative descriptions and no attributions for the speakers in this voice. Notice how I differentiated them above by italicizing Goose's words and leaving the farmer's words plain. In published books you might see one person's dialogue indented or one done in normal text and the other in italics.

When using the conversational voice, keep the different voices distinct. In the above example, notice Goose is untrusting throughout. On the other hand, the farmer is in a rush. He'll promise anything to get a look at that egg. Each voice must ring true to the character and help define him or her.

*Knots on a Counting Rope* by Bill Martin Jr. and John Archambault is a conversation between a little boy and his grandfather. The first two interactions go like this:

> Tell me the story again, Grandfather.
> Tell me who I am.

> I have told you many times, Boy.
> You know the story by heart.

Each time Grandfather talks his dialogue is indented.

*Being Friends* by Karen Beaumont opens with "I am me and you are you. I like red and you like blue." The story continues with one friend talking throughout about all their differences, but no matter how different they are, she knows they're the same because they both like to be friends.

# CORRESPONDENCE BETWEEN TWO CHARACTERS

Letters between two characters are another form of the conversation voice. Imagine the farmer posted this and then waited for his wife's response.

> Dear Wife,
> I'm writing with wonderful news.
> Goose laid a golden egg. I immediately rushed to town and deposited it in the bank.

> Dear Husband,
> I hope she laid more eggs. I must have a diamond bracelet. Earrings. And a necklace, too!

When creating a correspondence, you must concentrate on making each letter sound true to the character writing it, just as in dialogue you must work to make each character sound unique. These letters reveal the farmer as a practical man who quickly deposited the egg in a safe place. His wife, on the other hand, is already dreaming of how she will spend their riches. These letters introduce the beginning of a conflict between them.

Notice that a letter allows for compression of action and dialogue. In this tight construction you may summarize scenes and compress dialogue, because that is what we naturally do in letters.

*The Journey of Oliver K. Woodman* by Darcy Pattison is told entirely with letters, and it's not just between two people. It's a correspondence of several people! Uncle Ray in South Carolina cannot visit his niece Tameka in California, so he sends her a wooden friend named Oliver. He sets Oliver on the road with a note telling where he needs to go and asking whoever picks him up to send a note so Uncle Ray will know how the journey is going. What follows is a group of letters from different people describing where they picked up Oliver and a bit about their leg of the journey.

Here's another short quiz to see how well you can identify the apostrophe, mask, and conversation voices.

1. I am the house, empty and still.

2. Leaf, floating down the river, tell me of your travels.

3. "I hate you."
   "I know you don't mean that. Most children say that about their parents at one time or another."

4. Dog, what is so special about my furry slippers? Go chew on Mother's high-heeled shoes!

5. You're my sister. I'm the boss. You put the blocks away. Then we'll paint. You get blue. I get red.

6. "Please pass the pudding."
   "Get it yourself. I'm your brother, not your servant."

7. I lie on your floor, feeling your heavy footsteps, soaking up spills of hot cocoa and suffering the angry growls of your vacuum cleaner.

8. Dear Betty,
   Can you come to play?

   Dear Billy,
   Not today.

And the answers are: 1. mask 2. apostrophe 3. two-way conversation (notice how I establish who the characters are in the very beginning) 4. apostrophe (in this story the dog cannot talk back) 5. one-way conversation 6. two-way conversation 7. mask 8. conversation via two-way correspondence.

How did you do?

Experimenting with these different dramatic voices can open your eyes to new story possibilities. Any that you try will enrich and enliven your vision. Perhaps one of them will flick on a lightbulb in your head that says, "Perfect!" Follow that one to the end. The result will lift your story out of the ordinary and create something so unusual and compelling publishers will start a bidding war to buy it.

## WHAT'S NEXT?

I hope you've had fun experimenting with these unique approaches to writing your story, but you're not done yet. In chapter 5 we'll look at ways to open up new illustration possibilities. In addition, we'll also consider what happens when you change the tense of your story.

## BEFORE YOU GO ON

1. Rewrite the opening paragraph of your story in at least three of the following forms:
   a. Apostrophe voice
   b. Mask voice
   c. Conversation between two characters
   d. One-way conversation
   e. Two-way correspondence

2. Do you like any of these? If so, rewrite your entire story.

3. Read a new picture book.

# TELLING YOUR STORY
# —PART THREE

*Imagination is more important than knowledge.* —*Albert Einstein*

Following the lead of chapters 3 and 4, we will look at different ways to reimagine your story in chapter 5. The more you consider other possibilities for the manner of telling, the more likely you are to create an enduring book. Let's look at some final options

## CHANGING TENSES

We can see from the first sentence in the original version of *The Goose With the Golden Eggs*, "A farmer went to the nest of his goose to see whether she had laid an egg," that it was written in the past tense.

Now change it to the present tense and see what can happens.

> A farmer goes to the nest of his goose to see whether she had laid an egg. What's this?" he asks, holding the egg up close to his eyes. "I do believe this is gold." He shakes the egg. "Solid gold! I'm rich!" He rushes home to tell his wife.

Writing in the present tense can make your story more immediate to the reader. It's unfolding the same time the reader is reading it. This

increases the drama because the reader and listener are living it along with the character. No one knows what the ending will be.

*The Wall* by Eve Bunting takes place in the present tense. A little boy and his father are visiting the Vietnam Veterans Memorial in Washington, D.C. Because it's written as it happens, we see the flowers and flags and letters people have left just as the boy does. We are with him when he watches Dad put up a sheet of paper and rub it with a pencil so the letters of his grandfather's name show through. We feel the quiet when the class of children leaves the memorial.

What about the future tense?

> Tomorrow when the farmer goes to his goose's nest in search of an egg, he will be surprised. He will find not an ordinary eating egg, but a golden egg. Will he tell his wife? Will he keep the secret to himself?

*If You Give a Mouse a Cookie* by Laura Joffee Numeroff is a classic example of telling a story in the future tense. Whenever the boy does something to or for the mouse, he sets in motion a new action. Mouse will nap, or color, or maybe even clean the house.

## CHANGE THE TIME PERIOD IN WHICH YOUR STORY TAKES PLACE

If your story is told in the present day, perhaps you could change it to a previous time. *The Goose With the Golden Eggs* is already told in the past. What would happen if I moved it to the present?

> Mr. Smith, the owner of the biggest egg farm in the world, was inspecting his giant hen house. Thousands of hens stood squished together in small cages stacked from floor to ceiling. On every level a conveyor belt moved smoothly, carrying the eggs his hens had laid.
>
> Mr. Smith rubbed his hands in glee at all those smooth white eggs on their way to be packed in Styrofoam boxes. But wait! What was that?
> One egg was not white. It was golden!

48

Along with changing the goose into a hen, setting it in a different time creates all new picture possibilities. Remember, it's not enough to just change the time. You must integrate the aspects of this different world throughout.

We could also write this story in a future time:

> While speeding toward Mars, Astronaut Abraham opened his last packet of food. A dried egg? A dried golden egg? How could he eat that?

What about setting your contemporary story in colonial times? Earlier we talked about adding different levels to a story. A manuscript based in a historical period, if written well and accurately, will not only be a good story, but a teacher can use it when his students study that period.

*The Bat Boy & His Violin* by Gavin Curtis is story about a father and son with different interests and different dreams for the future. It could take place at any time but is infinitely enriched by the author's setting of 1948, with the Negro National League of Baseball playing a big part in their conflict.

# LOCATION OF YOUR STORY

We already changed locations when we moved our farmer to a big corporate farm. But you could move your city child into the country or your country child into the city. You could place your story in Zambia or Vietnam or Afghanistan. Any change in location will bring changes to your story. It will also require research to create an authentic setting, but the time will be well spent because your story will move out of the ordinary into the realm of extraordinary.

Ordinary cannot possibly make it in this world of more expensive paper and printing. It cannot make it in this world of increased competition and publishing house cutbacks. And it cannot make it in this world of the increasing price of picture books. You must make your manuscript so distinctive an editor will forget financial concerns and shout, "Yes! YES! **YES!**"

But we're not done yet.

# CHANGE HUMAN CHARACTERS INTO ANIMALS OR ANIMALS INTO PEOPLE

In *The Goose With the Golden Eggs*, I'm going to make the farmer a bear.

> "Grrrrrrr," growled Bear. "You'd better have laid me an egg today.
> I'm tired of eating my honey without scrambled eggs."
>   Goose trembles. "Yes, Bear. I did lay an egg today, but this
> isn't an egg you can eat."
>   "An egg is an egg," roared Bear. He shoved Goose away with
> his huge hairy paw.
>   His eyes grew big. "What's this?"

That tells a different story, doesn't it?

When is it a good idea to use animal characters instead of people?

Animal characters give your listeners an opportunity to distance themselves from the characters, especially when they are dealing with issues that might be too threatening and scary. My favorite example is *Owl Babies* by Martin Waddell. This story tells of owlets whose mother has left them, and they worry whether she will return. Imagine if he had written this about a little boy whose mother left and he didn't know if she would come back. The listener could identify with this and grow terrified. He, too, would worry about his mother leaving. When the main characters are owls, the listener doesn't readily see the connection. He is a safe distance from their problem. This is happening to someone different from him. Therefore, he doesn't have the same fears.

Another reason to switch to animal characters is that it allows for out-of-the-ordinary illustrations. *Ruby in Her Own Time* by Jonathan Emmett is about a duckling who is the last to hatch, slow to eat, and way behind her siblings when it comes to swimming. Eventually, of course, she does catch up to them and flies higher and wider and farther than all of them. This story could just as easily have been written about a child who lags behind his class, siblings, or friends, but pictures of a duck family are much more interesting than a human family!

If you have already told your story with animals, perhaps you should try telling your story with people. Let's suppose the goose is a poor servant girl. Obviously she can't lay an egg, but perhaps she brings back the eggs she has gathered.

"What's this?" the farmer asks.

"Goose's egg," the servant girl says. "It's solid gold. I found it in the hen house."

"You lie!" the farmer shouts. "You painted it gold in hopes I'll believe your silly story and give you the afternoon off."

You can change the verb tense, the time period, or the location of your story. You can even change the characters from people to animals or vice versa. But, as I'm typing this chapter, I've thought of other ways to tell a story … as a newspaper article, with recipe cards, e-mails, or text messages. I just read an adult book told entirely in footnotes! The possibilities are limited only by your imagination.

## WHAT'S NEXT?

Now that you know the many different ways you can tell your story, let's turn to your characters. Are they flat or three-dimensional? How do you create characters that children will remember all their lives?

## BEFORE YOU GO ON

1. Experiment with at least three ways of telling your story. Write the opening paragraph of each.

   a. Change the time of your story.
   b. Change the location of your story.

c. Change the verb tense of your story.

d. Change your characters to animals or vice versa.

2. If any of these pique your interest, rewrite the entire manuscript.

3. Read a new picture book.

# CHAPTER 6

# CREATING COMPELLING CHARACTERS

 *You can never know enough about*
*your characters. —W. Somerset Maugham*

Remember when you were the one listening to picture books? Which were your favorites? Did any have a character that continues to live on in your mind?

The best characters stay with readers and listeners long after childhood is over. That's why some books stay in print for generations—like Ferdinand from *The Story of Ferdinand* by Munro Leaf, Peter from *The Tale of Peter Rabbit* by Beatrix Potter, and Madeline from the book with the same title by Ludwig Bemelmans. These charming characters' books go on and on and are remembered with warmth and affection for generations. Sometimes people even name a child after a favorite storybook character.

I can still conjure up in my mind the picture of Ferdinand smelling those wonderful black-and-white flowers and refusing to fight. I can feel for Madeline looking small and forlorn in her bed at boarding school. I can also worry for Peter Rabbit sneaking into Farmer McGregor's garden. These long-ago characters remain with me to this day.

My children remember how Frances, from *Bedtime for Frances* by Russell Hoban, was terrified of the thump, thump of the butterfly's wings on her window, and how Curious George, from *Curious George Gets a Medal* by H.A. Rey, frantically tried to clean up the ink mess before his friend, the man with the yellow hat, returned. They still laugh over the cat, Rotten Ralph, in the book of the same name by Jack Gantos, sawing off the branch that held the swing with his owner Sarah in it!

Now we have a new generation of readers in love with David, from *No, David!* by David Shannon, who day and night hears nothing but "No!" They identify with exuberant Olivia, from the book of the same name by Ian Falconer, whose energy wears everyone out, even herself. My granddaughter loves playing dress-up like Nancy in *Fancy Nancy* by Jane O'Connor. These children will grow up to share their special books with their sons and daughters.

No doubt you have your own favorites. Look again at those memorable picture book characters. This time, study them as a writer, not as a reader or a listener. Think about the qualities that make a character stick with a picture book's audience long after the book is shut. The following attributes are important to me in a main character.

## SOMEONE YOU CARE ABOUT

I like a character that follows his or her dreams without regard to what others think. Wasn't it wonderful how Ferdinand refused to join in the bullfights? He gave me hope that I, too, could stand up for my convictions in spite of others' opinions. Perhaps you like a character like Chrysanthemum in Kevin Henkes's book titled after the main character, who is sympathetic because she is having doubts about her name, or the real-life Sarah Hale in *Thank You, Sarah: The Woman Who Saved Thanksgiving* by Laurie Halse Anderson, who never gave up through many obstacles and years to achieve her goal of getting Thanksgiving proclaimed a national holiday. Think about the characters that touch an emotional chord with you. Perhaps you should write about that type of character.

## CHARACTERS NEED TO BE LIKABLE

It's hard to feel compassion for a bully. Who wants to read about someone who is always trying to make others feel small? We cheer for Owen in the book *Owen* by Kevin Henkes because he insists on his right to carry his blanket in spite of adult disapproval. Do we cheer for the nosy neighbor Mrs. Scissors, who does all she can to encourage his parents to make him stop? I think not.

However, even a bully, if you give him a trait that makes him not all bad, can turn into a sympathetic character. In *The Recess Queen*, Alexis O'Neill makes Mean Jean likable when she lets readers know that no one ever played with her. At that point we realize her behavior might have stemmed from, or been the cause of, no one asking her to play—surely a sad circumstance. We feel a connection with her loneliness.

# A CHILD, ADULT, OR ANIMAL THAT IS CHILDLIKE

Peter Rabbit is a child in fur. Farmer Brown in *Click, Clack, Moo: Cows That Type* is childlike in wanting his way no matter what.

Of course, there are exceptions to every rule. *Harriet, You'll Drive Me Wild!* by Mem Fox is one of them. Although Harriet is the first character onstage, the book is more about the mother's increasing frustration with her daughter to the point where she finally loses her temper and YELLS! In general, however, children prefer to read about themselves or characters similar to them.

# IMPERFECT

We *all* have flaws. Our characters must have flaws, too. Haven't we all disobeyed our parents like Peter Rabbit? Haven't we all paid the consequences? And aren't we still loved by our parents no matter what?

Haven't we all lacked confidence like Chrysanthemum?

And haven't we all misbehaved so much that we, too, heard "No! No! No!" just like David?

Think about your imperfections. Think about imperfections in others that annoy you or maybe tug at your heart. When it comes to writing, I'm very driven. That drive compels me to sit at my computer every day. It prods me to rarely give up on a story. And it insists

I keep learning my craft. I see my drive as a strength, but maybe my husband doesn't. He might wish I spent more time with him. When my kids were young, they might have seen my drive as selfish, especially when I wasn't 100 percent thrilled to help them with their studies, practice soccer, or bake cookies for their swim meets.

Often as with my drive/selfishness, the strength and weakness are two sides of the same issue. Think of Frances in Russell Hoban's *Bedtime for Frances*. Her great imagination is exactly what makes her so fearful. It's what makes her sure spiders and tigers and monsters lurk in her room.

Whatever the specifics, the main characters in our picture books must be human, and that means imperfect.

## BEHAVE IN BELIEVABLE WAYS

Your characters are not robots whose behavior is controlled by a computer (or an author). Their actions are not driven by the plot or the writer's whims.

Suppose you have written about an incredibly shy character that stands at the back of a crowd and always lets others lead the way. One day, for no apparent reason, that shy girl storms to the front of the class and leads a march demanding chocolate cake for lunch every day. This *might* work if we saw her change along the way, by slowly, subtly taking more action. If it happens all of a sudden, it feels completely out of character.

Emily in *Loud Emily* by Alexis O'Neill doesn't ever speak in a soft voice. It wouldn't be like her to do so. She is born with a loud voice and uses that voice throughout the story, and in the end, to great advantage.

## THE MAIN CHARACTER MUST BE ACTIVE, NOT PASSIVE

Even Ferdinand's defiant act of sitting and refusing to fight was active because he took a stand for what mattered to him. Mary Veronica in *Mary Veronica's Egg* by Mary Nethery insists throughout the book that her egg will hatch something special like a dinosaur or an alligator! Although she doesn't win a prize for the Most Unusual Pet at the school pet fair, she knows that her baby duckling is "the best prize of all."

Lucy in *Go to Bed, Monster!* by Natasha Wing loves to draw. She draws a monster, but he doesn't scare her. She draws castles for them to play in, airplanes to fly, and a parade to march in. They have great fun together until Lucy grows tired. Unfortunately, the monster doesn't want to go to bed. More drawing by Lucy finally gets the Monster to sleep so she can sleep, too. Each character is active in his or her own way.

# MAIN CHARACTER SOLVES HER OWN PROBLEM

Admit it, doesn't it bother you if someone says, "You should do it this way," especially when you haven't asked for the advice? All day long, a teacher, babysitter, parent, older sibling, grandparent, relative, neighbor—you name it—is telling children what they should do.

Successful parents let children struggle to solve manageable problems. These solutions enable their children to take on more grown-up tasks with confidence. When the characters in our stories solve their own problems (in appropriate childlike ways), we send an empowering message to our young listeners. In *Go to Bed, Monster!*, Lucy keeps drawing. Mother doesn't come in and suggest, "Why don't you draw a bed for Monster? What about reading him a story?" Lucy comes up with these ideas by herself.

So, let's summarize.

We want our characters in our picture book stories to be:

1. someone the reader cares about.
2. likable.
3. a child, or an adult, or animal who is childlike.
4. an imperfect character.
5. someone who behaves in ways believable to that character.
6. active, not passive.
7. able to solve their own problems.

Sound easy? If it were, we would all be writing stories editors would snap up. And all our published books would become bestsellers. Unfortunately creating compelling characters takes time, thought, and work.

## HOW TO CREATE UNIQUE, MEMORABLE, AND CONSISTENT CHARACTERS

We have to **know our characters inside and out.** It is not enough to have a general picture of a character in your head when you start writing. I learned the hard way. Who, I thought, wants to spend time composing a character study? Better to just write the story.

Wrong!

When working with my editor, Melanie Kroupa, on *Everything to Spend the Night,* she asked me if I'd made a character study of the little girl. I said, "Yes," but she probably sensed the tentativeness in my voice. She asked me to send it to her. Quickly I wrote two or three sentences and e-mailed them off.

She called back and said that wasn't nearly enough.

She was right.

I went back to my computer and wrote an in-depth character study that consumed much time and several pages. Only then did I discover that my character loved to play games, was full of energy, and thrilled to be at Grandpa's house. Once I had my character firmly in my mind, the rewriting was easy. I knew she would pack jacks and puzzles and drums in her bag. She was imaginative and would bring lots of things to play queen. Although I always pack a book, often several, when I go away, I knew my character would not do the same thing. She was way too active for a book. It made me sad not to have the story end with the little girl and Grandpa reading together. However, whenever I autograph this book, I write "Always pack a book," and now you know why.

That positive experience of the value of a character study was the kick-in-the-pants I needed to get over my fear and avoidance of creating characters and their studies. So many things on first glance appear complicated yet turn out to be easy and fun. That's the way it is with creating a character. You get to play God. This little boy, girl, bear, or bunny is entirely yours. Granted, forming well-rounded characters takes time—but not as much as you'd think. And it's time more than well spent.

Perhaps I do my character study first. Or I might wait until I have a first draft down; then I pause, fill out my character study, and go back and revise with the personality, backstory, and emotions of my character firmly in mind. The critical thing is to do a study *sometime*.

Today I would never submit a manuscript without having written a character study. I make studies for each character that appears in my story and refer to them often.

Don't panic! Obviously a character that speaks only a line or two will have a less in-depth study. Sometimes just knowing a strong personality trait is enough for minor characters.

How do I make the study for my main character?

I fill in the information called for on a form I keep permanently in my computer. It's simple, gleaned from many lists I've read in various books and suggestions I've heard at conferences over the years. Most of these lists from books and conferences were unduly long and way too detailed for a picture book character. That's why I've tinkered with the different lists and whittle mine down to just five items. It works for me, and I hope it will work for you.

So here goes.

# FIVE THINGS YOU MUST KNOW ABOUT YOUR PICTURE BOOK CHARACTER

## 1. Name

What's in a name? A lot! Alexis O'Neill named her character in *The Recess Queen* Mean Jean. Would Mean Alice have the same impact? What kind of character might you name Amanda, which comes from the Latin, meaning "worthy of love?" Would you name a happy-go-lucky child Miriam, from the Hebrew meaning "sea of sorrow, or bitterness?"

What type of character might have the hard-sounding name Curt? What kind of personality might a boy have to be named Misha, with its soft sounds? Or should you go against the expected and name the gentle character Curt and the tough guy Misha? Names should be word pictures of the character. While discussing names, here's the fastest way to get your story noticed by an editor for the *wrong* reasons. Call your characters, like I did in one of my earlier stories, Sammy Skunk and Billy Beaver. Alliterative names shout out "cute" and "lack of respect for the child listener." They make it easy for the editor to drop your story in the form rejection pile.

What's the matter with calling your characters Skunk and Beaver? In *Mañana, Iguana*, my characters were named Iguana, Tortuga (the Spanish word for turtle), Culebra (the Spanish word for snake), and Conejo (the Spanish word for rabbit). Imagine if I'd named them Ida Iguana, Tommy Tortuga, Cathy Culebra, and Connie Conejo!

A good rule of thumb is to call the animals simply *Fox, Mole, Hare, Otter,* and *Squirrel,* as Alan Durant does in his touching book *Always and Forever,* which deals with coming to terms with death. Or give the character the human name *Owen* like Kevin Henkes did, and then he drew him as a mouse.

Another thing you need to keep in mind is not to give characters names that might confuse the child listener. Names that are too similar like Matthew and Martin probably belong in separate stories.

The name of your character will most likely call forth a picture of the sex of the child, unless you are trying to keep it ambiguous for the illustrator. For example, Laura McGee Kvasnosky's *Zelda and Ivy* is obviously not about two boys. However, if you named a character after my friend and Newbery Honor-winning author Kirby Larson, it might not be so clear. She frequently gets mail addressed to Mr. Kirby Larson.

Does your character have a nickname? What does it say about your character? How was it bestowed?

# 2. Birth Date and Age at the Time of the Story

The birth date helps set your story in a certain time period. For example, a five-year-old child born in 1700 will be very different from a five-year-old born in the year 2000.

If you write about a child born in the mid 1700s you would be able to use words like *carriage, blacksmith* and *hornbook*—words you wouldn't have chosen if your character were born in our current century.

Age at the time of the story is critical. What are the characteristics of the age of your character? A two-year-old behaves unlike a four-year-old or an eight-year-old.

Does your character act his or her age? Does he speak baby talk? Does he try to act tough like his big brother? How old do others see your character?

## 3. Appearance

Maybe your character is an animal. This is where to describe that. Looks are important for you to know. Sometimes when I'm working, I keep a photograph of my character in front of me. I get this from family snapshots or magazine and newspaper photos. Note that this description or image of your character is only for you. The illustrator may paint a character far removed from what you imagine. However, having a picture in your mind, whether it matches the illustrator's or not, makes for stronger writing.

Does your character spend a lot of time on appearance or is it of little consequence? Does he want to look like someone else? Is she neat? Is he sloppy? What kind of clothes might she wear? Does he have favorite clothes?

Health might be important here, too. Is your character sickly? Does she have a limp? Perhaps he is autistic.

## 4. Relationships With Others

Start first with the family, especially if they are an important part of the story. Who are the parents, siblings, and extended family? It's not enough to just give names here. What are they like? Provide descriptions, personalities, etc. Are there any problems your character has with them? Is the family from a foreign country? Do they have activities and beliefs unique to their original culture? If so, what are they? How comfortable are they adjusting to their new land?

Is family income relevant to your story? Do both parents work? How does that impact your character?

What about friends? Neighbors? Teachers? If they play a part in the story, we need to know your main character's interactions and feelings about them.

# 5. Personality

I've saved the most important area to focus on for last. It might help you to look at some picture books you love and think about the characters in them. How would you define the personality of the mouse in Laura Joffe Numeroff's *If You Give a Mouse a Cookie*? Does the mouse have the same personality as Grace in Karen Winnick's *Mr. Lincoln's Whiskers*? What makes them dissimilar? How do these characters compare with Babar? Differentiating between characters in published books will help you better define your own characters.

In this section of my study, I want to know my character's strengths and weaknesses, his attitudes, fears, obsessions, special talents and hobbies. I think about whether she might have a favorite phrase like "Go for it," or a habit of running her fingers through her hair whenever she's bored. This is also the place where I try to hear my character's voice. I pretend I am the character and write a letter to me, the author, about what happens in the story and his feelings about it.

So, that's it! Just five simple categories to explore:

- Name
- Birth date and age at time of story
- Appearance
- Relationships with others
- Personality

Now that you're done, don't save your study in a file or store it in a drawer to be forgotten. Go back and reread it. You may even revise it a bit, deleting, changing, or clarifying things.

If I'm in the process of writing a story or it's just an idea in my head, when I'm at my computer and have a question about the character's behavior, I reread my study. If I'm away from a story for a while, I also reread it before getting back to work.

With the character study firmly in mind, you can pause in your revising and ask: Would my character speak in that manner? Based on what you now know about him, you might realize he would act differently than you initially thought.

However, always leave room in your writing for surprises. Characters may suddenly say or do something startling. Writers often talk about the joy of following a character's unexpected lead, and that's fine. Just make sure that before you send off your story to an editor, your final version shows your character acting appropriately and consistently with his personality.

You might feel the above five items are not enough. Maybe you've completed them and need to delve deeper into your character before you write or revise. If so, here are two other areas, specific to the action of your story, to think about.

## 1. What has brought the character to this point in the start of the story?

Something has probably happened to bring the character to the time your story begins. Describe this in detail. For example, my book *Tortuga in Trouble* begins with Tortuga ready to set off with a basket of food for his *abuela*, or grandmother. I know that before the story began he learned she was not feeling well, and that's why he's going to visit her. I also know Tortuga moves slowly, and he's gotten burned by his friends in the past so he is not trusting of their motives now. None of this needed to go into the finished version, but it definitely enriched my connection and understanding of Tortuga at the opening of the story.

## 2. What does the main character want?

Does he want to get over his fear of the dark? Does she want to learn how to ride a tricycle?

If the main character is going to get what she wants, what must the character overcome? Is it a bully? Her own shyness? Is it having to convince her parents of something?

One more thing you should remember: Because picture books are short and written for children who are new to books, we write our books with **just one main character.**

Many of you are probably wondering about *Owl Babies* by Martin Waddell, which has the three owlets: Sarah, Percy, and Bill. First of all, you will find exceptions to almost any statements, or instructions, about writing.

However, I don't think this is an exception. Even though there are three characters, each represents an expression of the many sides of one character. When Mother goes away, we're hopeful she'll return (like Sarah); we're worried something bad might happen (like Percy); and we ache with love (like Bill).

If you have more than one main character in a book, make sure they act and sound unique from one another. I faced this problem with my books *Mañana, Iguana; Fiesta Fiasco; Count on Culebra;* and *Tortuga in Trouble*. Many hours were spent creating each one. To summarize their longer studies, Iguana is the active one who is always making plans and organizing things. She loves parties and cooking for friends. Self-centered Conejo will do anything to get out of work. He's also a trickster. Culebra is more of a tease who likes to play jokes. He's also the most cerebral. Tortuga is the slow and steady one—he's also a tad insecure and can be swayed by others.

Having these characteristics firmly in my mind makes it easy for me to recognize when one character is speaking in the voice of another.

Once you have made your studies and think each of your characters is distinctive, it's time to test whether each one does, in fact, act according to his or her personality.

# TESTING YOUR CHARACTER FOR CONSISTENCY

The best way to do this is to print a hard copy of your manuscript, then move away from your computer to your desk or a comfortable chair. With a single colored highlighter, mark every dialogue and action of your main character. When you've completed that, take a *different* colored highlighter and do the same for another character. If you have more than two, highlight the speech and actions of each one with a new color.

Then go through the manuscript and read out loud only one color from beginning to end. This allows you to see and hear when and where they are speaking and acting in ways that are out of character. It gives you a throughline, removing the distractions of the other characters.

Now you know the kind of characters we want in children's books and how to create a well-rounded one in your study. You also know how to use highlighters to test if your character is acting and speaking consistently.

## WHAT'S NEXT?

You've created a unique and engaging character. It's time to take a look at structural storytelling issues. First of all, the important opening. If your story doesn't start out strong, no one will ever get to read your fabulous middle and ending.

## BEFORE YOU GO ON

1. Make a character study for each of your characters.

2. With a clean copy of your manuscript, get out a different colored highlighter for each character. Go through the manuscript one character at a time. Highlight whenever that character speaks and/or acts. If you try to do too many characters at the same time, shifting from one color to the other, I guarantee you will make a mistake at least once.

3. Now read only the dialogue and actions of one of those colors. Does everything your character says sound true to her? What about her actions? If not, rewrite.

4. Did you notice one character, or maybe several, who appear in the beginning but not in the end, or vice versa? If so, they probably aren't necessary to your story. Try deleting them or perhaps combining them with another character.

5. Read a new picture book.

STRUCTURE OF YOUR STORY

# DIVING INTO YOUR STORY

*The first lines of a story teach us
how to read it.* —John L'Heureux

Are you uneasy when it comes to writing your picture book opening? Do you start as I used to, by describing your character's personality and appearance, the location, the weather, before finally, on the second or maybe even the third page, getting to the character's problem? Don't be a nervous swimmer, testing your story waters with your toe. Dive right in.

You don't have lots of time in this busy world to grab your reader's attention, much less an editor's—the most important first reader of your manuscript. How long will an editor give you before she tosses your story into the rejection pile? Most admit the first few paragraphs show them all they need to know about the potential of a story.

Picture book writers don't have the novelist's luxury to creep into a story. Your opening has to be quick, grabbing the audience from the get-go.

## WHAT MAKES A STRONG OPENING?

A strong opening contains six *W*s.

# Who Is Your Main Character?

In picture books, the main character must come on stage first. If you start with a secondary character, you'll confuse the listener. She isn't sure with whom to identify.

But it's not enough for the main character to come on stage first if he doesn't step on in a lively manner. The writer needs to start with a scene and let us meet the main character through dialogue, action, or another's reaction to him.

That's exactly what Bethany Roberts does in *A Mouse Told His Mother*. It opens with Mouse telling his mother that he is planning on taking a trip. We need to go no farther than the first line to know the main character is Mouse. We hear him in a scene talking with Mother. He wants to go on a trip, so we learn he is adventurous. Roberts does not start out by telling us Mouse loved adventure. She shows us by his dialogue.

# What Does Your Character Want?

What is the main character's problem, goal, or conflict? In *A Chair for Baby Bear*, Kaye Umansky begins her story this way:

> "When are you going to fix my chair, Papa," asks Baby Bear.

Easy enough, isn't it? Baby Bear wants Papa to fix his chair.

The conflict comes in the second line when Papa Bear says, "Soon, Baby Bear." We learn further on that Papa Bear said the same thing yesterday and the day before, and the conflict grows larger as the story unfolds.

Conflicts can be divided into four categories.

## Conflict With Oneself

In this type of conflict, the main character needs to overcome some lack in herself, such as fear of the dark, difficulty sharing toys, jealousy over a new baby or, as Marla Frazee's little girl in *Roller Coaster*, conquering her terror of her first roller coaster ride. Once Frazee's character starts zipping and zooming, she gets over her fear so much that the last line reads:

But at least one of them (the passengers) is planning to ride the roller coaster again ... right now!

## Conflict With Others

Conflict with others means your main character must come to terms with another character—perhaps with a bully at nursery school, or with Father insisting he go to the grocery store with him, or with a friend who wants to play in the sandbox instead of on the swings.

Lynne Jonell writes about conflict with others in *It's My Birthday, Too!*, a story of a big brother who doesn't want his little brother at his birthday party. It opens with big brother, Christopher, telling little brother, Robby, that he is having a birthday party. Robby says that he's allowed to attend. With hilarious consequences, Robbie gets Christopher to agree that he can come to the party if he's a puppy.

## Conflict With the Larger World

In this conflict, your character has issues with a group in the community. Stories of this sort might include your character convincing the government that a stoplight is needed at her school crossing, or trying to put a halt to a freeway from being built through her backyard, or insisting the city enforce leash laws so a big dog wouldn't attack her. Margaree King Mitchell, in her touching book Uncle Jed's Barbershop, has (among other things) discrimination, segregation, and the Great Depression standing in the way of Uncle Jed's dream to own a barbershop. But he persists and finally, at the age of seventy-nine, opens it. Sadly he dies soon after that, but the ending is upbeat because Mitchell wrote that Uncle Jed died content because he lived his dream and he inspired the author to follow her dreams also.

## Conflict With Nature

Here the character is not battling himself, a person, or persons or the larger world, but nature. Perhaps a swimmer is struggling against strong tides, or a child is shoveling snow in a snowstorm and nothing he does can keep the walk clean. Maybe a tornado rips through a town.

In *River Friendly, River Wild,* Jane Kurtz writes about the changes brought to a young girl and her family when the river near their home overflowed its banks and they were forced to evacuate.

> We rush—
> hush—
> through the midnight streets
> out of the silent city
> away from the river
> away from home.

Of course, some picture books don't have a character with a problem to solve. These are concept books where the writer explores a subject. Nevertheless, the reader still needs to know right away what the book is about.

In my picture book mentioned earlier, *Hello Toes! Hello Feet!*, the opening lines said:

> Good morning, toes,
> Good morning, feet,
> tangled up between my sheets.

It's obvious that this book is going to be about toes and feet. Consider what might happen if I reversed the sentence and starting talking about sheets first.

> Sheets? Stop twisting around my feet!

The reader would then be confused with my next line ...

> Be the first to touch the floor,
> Hop me to the closet door.

Hey! They'd wonder. Is this about sheets, or is it about feet?

## When Is Your Story Taking Place?

Sometimes the writer will want to give the exact date and time of the story. However, that's not always necessary. Contemporary stories can leave the date and year unstated. If your story takes place in a different time, you can give hints by the use of character names

indicative of that period, unusual or old-fashioned phrasing, or by mentioning an object special to that time. Karen Winnick, in *Mr. Lincoln's Whiskers*, writes on her first page:

> Grace flew down the porch steps. "Papa, how was the fair?" she asked. "Did you meet Mr. Lincoln?"
> "No, Grace," Papa said. "Abraham Lincoln didn't come here to New York. He's remaining in Springfield, Illinois, during the election."

By mentioning Abraham Lincoln, the election, and the fact that he was remaining in Springfield, we (at least the adult reader) will know this story is probably taking place in 1859 before Lincoln's first election to the presidency. The use of *Papa* rather than *Dad* or *Father* is another hint to the time period.

## Where Is Your Story Taking Place?

Just as the reader and listener need to be grounded in the story's time period, they also should know where the story is taking place. Is it in a city, the country, or the suburbs? Does it take place in England, Iran, or China?

You don't have to set the scene with long and lovely descriptions. If I wanted to write a book about a farmer, I wouldn't start my story by saying,

> On a farm in Wisconsin with picket fences around the field and a big gray barn.

No. I would just say:

> Farmer Jack is in mess of trouble.

The use of the word *Farmer* is all we need to know. The illustrator, can then decide what the farm will look like. Maybe he'll paint the barn white and draw a chain-link fence.

## What Is the Tone of Your Story?

Is your story going to be funny? Serious? Sad? How do you let the reader know what lies ahead?

Your careful selection of words and rhythms lets the reader know. (We'll discuss this in depth in chapters 13 and 14.) Give clues for a funny story by writing playful, perhaps even made-up, words. Use upbeat, happy rhythms in your sentences.

April Halprin Wayland's *It's Not My Turn to Look for Grandma!* begins like this:

> Dawn was just cracking over the hills. Ma was splitting kindling on the back porch.
> "Woolie!" she called out. "Where in the hickory stick is Grandma?
> "Dunno," said Woolie. "It's not my turn to look for Grandma!"
> It was Mack's turn.

The hard sounds of Wayland's first paragraph—*cracking, kindling, back,* and *porch*—show us this is not going to be a quiet book. Then she gave a boy a fun name of Woolie. What about her phrase, "Where in the hickory stick …"? Doesn't that make you smile? And then Woolie answers with "Dunno."

Wayland has let us know immediately that we're in for a fun ride with this story.

Because setting the tone is so important, let's look again at the first two lines of my book *Hello Toes! Hello Feet!*

> Good morning, toes,
> Good morning, feet
> tangled up between my sheets.

Notice the hard *G, T* and *B* sounds. The reader will be jolted by their loudness and expect a lively book. The upbeat iambic rhythm (one soft beat and then a stress) promises a happy story also. Don't be discouraged if *iambi* is a foreign word to you. Poetry will be your friend by the time you finish this book.

More serious stories would make use of softer word sounds and falling rhythms. Perhaps the sentences would be longer, too. Compare the openings above to Amy MacDonald's in *The Spider Who Created the World*:

> When the sky was
> young and the world

just a dream, when
the stars were still
learning their names,
a spider named Nobb
came floating through
the Air, at the end
of a long, soft thread.

Here we have one long sentence with lots of soft *O*s and *N*s and *M*s. Quiet sounds for the beginning of a quiet story.

Karen Hesse uses rhythm in the first sentence of *The Cats in Krasinski Square*:

The cats
come
from the cracks in the Wall,
the dark corners,
the openings in the rubble.

The last two lines suggest heaviness because both end with falling rhythm words. That means the stress comes first and then the soft sound. Also, hear the repetition of the hard *C* sounds. There's an ominous quality of the hard *C*s combined with the falling rhythms. This is not a story that is going to make the reader laugh.

# WOW!

This is where you hook the reader, like a fisherman hooks a fish, so she can't close the book until she's reached the end. It can be a word or a phrase. It can come when you meet the character or when you hear the problem. But it must appear somewhere early. Look at the opening for *Thank You, Sarah: The Woman Who Saved Thanksgiving* by Laurie Halse Anderson. In just her fourth sentence she declares that we might have lost Thanksgiving.

No wonder this story was made into a book. Who wouldn't be intrigued by the idea that we almost didn't have Thanksgiving? What a *Wow!* moment! We have to read more.

Because this *Wow!* factor is so important, let's look at a few more examples.

This is from the book *George Washington's Teeth* by Deborah Chandra and Madeleine Comora.

> The Revolutionary War
> George hoped would soon be won,
> But another battle with his teeth
> Had only just begun ...

This first verse wows me because I'm curious about a battle I never knew George Washington waged—a battle with his teeth!

Here's another strong *Wow!* from *Dadblamed Union Army Cow* by Susan Fletcher. It comes in the second sentence.

> That dadblamed cow!
> When I went to join
> the Union Army,
> she did not stay home
> like a regular cow,
> but followed me down
> to the enlistment office.

And there's certainly a *Wow!* moment in the beautiful *Owl Babies* by Martin Waddell when the owlets waken and realize their mother has left them all alone. Any young listener would sit up with a jerk hearing that Mother is gone.

# TESTING FOR A STRONG OPENING

How do you discover if your opening contains all 6 *W*s and whether they come close to the beginning of your story?

Here's a test that gives you the visual, colorful picture of how soon your opening includes all it needs. I prefer highlighters for this test, but crayons, colored pencils, or colored pens work, too.

So you can see this in action, here is an early draft of an opening for one of my stories.

It was late at night. Mother held up Alan's pajamas. "It is time for bed."

"No, no, no," said Alan. "First I have to brush my teeth."

Alan brushed his teeth.

"Now," said Mother. "Let me put on your pajamas."

Mother slipped Alan's pajamas on. "Now it's time for bed."

"First you need to read me a story." Alan snuggled under his sheets.

Mother read him a story. She closed the book. Then she turned off the light. And tucked him in tight. "Good night, Alan."

"Good night?" Alan jumped out of bed. "I forgot to say, 'good night' to Father."

Let's see how well my opening passes the color test. Start with red to mark the place that lets the reader know **Who is the main character.**

Mother is the first one on stage, so you might think she is the main character. However, since this is a children's book, we should assume this story is about Alan. I'm not really sure. Is it Mother's problem that Alan doesn't want to go to bed or is it Alan's problem? We'll have to wait and read more. Thus there's no red mark for character on this story.

Does the opening do any better with the yellow highlighter, marking the words that tell **What the character wants?**

We know Mother wants Alan to go to bed. We know from Alan putting roadblocks in the way that he doesn't want to go to bed. But again we have trouble because we're not sure whose story this is. I would hold off with a yellow mark here, too.

Let's go on to the green highlighter. This is to indicate the words that show **When the story is taking place.**

Here I've done much better. The very first line tells us "It was late at night." So I would mark *late at night* with my green highlighter. However, I would make a note to myself that it's a pretty boring way of indicating night. Perhaps I should revise this later, but I'm happy to have at least one color on my opening.

Time to try the blue highlighter to mark **Where the story is taking place.**

This, too, might be a color. I assume this story takes place in a house because Alan wants to brush his teeth and he climbs into bed. Of course, he could be in a hotel or an apartment. I'm not sure if it matters whether this story is located in the city or the country, or even if it's in an apartment instead of a house. I guess I would highlight "Alan brushed his teeth." But I wouldn't be happy with it. A house is a mundane location, especially when it comes to pictures. Many stories take place at home. I jot down another note to myself: *Consider a more unique setting.* Up to this point, my opening has done so-so on the test. But with two more *W*s and two more colors, I maintain hope to further brighten my paper. The purple marker is to tell the reader **What the tone of the story is.**

Oh, no! I flunked terribly here. We start with a bedtime story that almost always feels sweet, especially when Mother tucks him in tight. But there's also some tension in the story because of Alan's dillydallying. The reader is going to have to read more to decide on the tone.

So far I only have two colors, and neither of them is very strong. I'm down to the last highlighter—the most important one. Orange should mark the words that make the reader want to say **Wow!**

Do you get a *Wow!* here? Do you want to read any farther?

I don't. Bedtime stories are a dime a dozen, and so far this one has nothing intriguing enough to make me want to go on.

Fortunately I took the color test before I sent the manuscript out. It showed me I had work to do. A lot of work!

After much thought and many hours revising, here is the opening to the same story. You may recognize it as the start of my published book *Little Monkey Says Good Night.*

> "Come, Little Monkey," Papa Monkey says. "The sky is dark. The moon is high. It's time for bed."
>
> Little Monkey shakes his head. "First I need to say good night."
> He scampers to the Big Top Tent.

You'll notice some big changes were made. I turned my son Alan into a monkey, and I let Papa Monkey put him to bed unlike the usual mother-child bedtime book. Doing those two things has already improved my story by giving the illustrator many more fun picture possibilities. The reader knows right away this isn't an ordinary good-night story. Let's apply the color test ...

How does the opening do now?

Much better!

The six *W*s are answered right away. Little Monkey is the first one mentioned so we know he's the main character. Do we know anything about him? Yes. He's not obedient when he shakes his head, and he's also full of energy by the selection of the word *scamper* to de-scribe the way he goes to the Big Top Tent. And we definitely know what Little Monkey wants. He wants to say good night.

The story still takes place at night, but this time it's told in a more lyrical way than in the first version.

> The sky is dark. The moon is high.

And now the story's setting is in a circus. We know that when Little Monkey scampers off to the Big Top Tent. The language indicates a light, energetic tone. There's the repetition of sentence form in Papa's description of night. The rhythm in these sentences is another iambic, one of the upbeat rhythms you'll learn about in chapter 13. Additionally, a rhyme is thrown in with *bed* and *head*. Yes, this definitely feels like a fun good-night story.

The use of hard-sounding letters like *T* and *B* and *D* and *P* and hard *C* also let the reader know this is not going to be the usual quiet good-night book. It starts out noisy and continues that way throughout.

And *Wow* When Little Monkey scampers off to the Big Top Tent, most readers want to read on and see what happens to him.

Obviously, having all the information as close to the beginning as possible is best. Sometimes, though, information may be found in the illustrations and does not need to be spelled out in the text. And as you will have noticed in the example from my *Little Monkey* book, sometimes the highlighter colors overlap. For instance, the *Wow!* moment also came when we marked the setting.

## WHAT'S NEXT?

We've covered the characteristics of a strong opening, but we haven't touched on that critical first line. That comes in chapter 8.

## BEFORE YOU GO ON

1. Apply the color test to your own manuscript. How successful is your opening? Can you do better? If so, revise.

Sometimes you might want to do this exercise with another writer. You'll need two copies of your story so you can each mark the opening separately. Then compare the two marked manuscripts. Are the colors in the same place? Perhaps the *Wow!* moment you marked comes much later to your outside reader. Again, it's time to revise.

2. Print clean copies of your two published manuscripts and apply the color test to each opening. Perhaps the weak opening is the reason for the bad manuscript. Is the opening strong in the good picture book?

Comparing the color tests of your story to successful published books can be both humbling and educational. In the future, type up the script of any new favorite picture book and apply the color test to it. The more you understand how published writers create strong openings, the more you'll be able to do the same with yours.

3. Read a new picture book.

78

# CREATING A
# FABULOUS FIRST LINE

*The first line of a poem is a hawk which
won't let go of its prey.* —*Gabriel Preil*

Since picture books have many similarities to poetry this quote definitely applies to us. Like poets, we must bait our readers with a sharp hook from the first line.

Attend a writing workshop with Richard Peck and you no doubt will hear him say, *"You're only as good as your opening line."*

Here are a few first lines that would make me want to read more:

> Baker Jake slammed his fist on the counter. "Oh, no!" he moaned.

*Wow!* What's happened to upset him so? Did he drop his eggs and now they're all cracked and ruined? Did the wedding cake he made fall into something no thinner than a sheet of paper? Maybe a new bakery opened next door. Regardless, wouldn't you want to turn the page and find out?

> What would it be like to be a giraffe?

It's intriguing to think about this question from a giraffe's point of view. What does he see with his head so high above the trees? Does he have conversations with birds? Does he sleep standing up?

Or perhaps:

> Mother told me after supper that we've lost everything and have to move.

I'm curious. Why did they lose everything? What will happen now? Will she have to move in with her least favorite cousin? Maybe they'll live in their car? Maybe they'll go to a homeless shelter?

And one last example:

> If a book wagon stopped at the beach
> what would those creatures
> who lived in the sea
> choose to read?

Might Lobster pick a book about anger management? Perhaps Starfish will choose one about the constellations in the sky. And Whale? Maybe the latest diet book. I want to find out.

In your future reading, pay attention to the first lines of everything you read. Does one work exceptionally well? Does another fall flat? Take time to consider why.

Successful first lines make it feel as if those lines were so right and natural they wrote themselves. But I suspect each author spent many hours experimenting with different ones. You will have to do the same.

What makes a great first line?

In our last chapter we discussed the importance of the *Wow!* moment coming early. If you can get that *Wow!* moment in the first line, you will have hooked the reader right off the bat. Joni Sensel, who writes books for older readers, suggests writers start with a Bang—or with an Axe. When creating a great first line, experiment with your focus. There are eight different ways to approach it.

To see how this works, I'm going to rewrite the first line from *The Story of the Three Little Pigs*. The opening sentence from a collection of English fairy tales, collected by Joseph Jacobs, reads:

> There was an old sow with three little pigs, and as she had not enough to keep them, she sent them out to seek their fortune.

# TIME

Traditionally the writer might start with "Once upon a time," "Long ago and far away," or "When pigs could talk." Each of these is fine, but all are old-fashioned. I might open with:

> It had been three days since the old sow sent her little pigs out to seek their fortune.

This sentence would indicate desperation in not having found their fortunes yet, so tension would be increased. What are the little pigs going to do?

# MOOD

If I want to set a sad mood, I would focus on the sow.

> The old sow blinked away tears as her three little pigs disappeared down the road ... forever.

What reader wouldn't feel compassion for that poor mother and want to read more? But since we know this is really the three little pigs' story, what about this?

> The three little pigs clicked their hooves and skipped down the road to seek their fortunes.

Or maybe they aren't happy. Maybe they have some doubts.

> The three little pigs lingered for a long while saying their last good-byes to Mother.

# SETTING

For this story, I might focus on the poverty of the setting. Obviously if the mother could, she would keep her children close to her.

> Anyone who saw the old sow's house with its saggy roof, peeling paint, and broken windows knew she couldn't feed her three little pigs much longer.

Or perhaps the setting isn't so terrible ...

> At the end of the lane, under the tall oak tree, the old sow waved goodbye to her three little pigs.

# OPINION

Sometimes, especially with a strong, compelling narrator, the first line can open with an opinion. Here's a negative one:

> What on earth could that old sow have been thinking, sending her three little pigs to find their fortunes alone in the cruel world?

Here's a more upbeat point of view:

> How wonderful that Mother Sow had enough faith in her children to send them off on their own, full of confidence that all will be well!

Or what about focusing on the three little pigs?

> Some pigs will do anything they can to avoid work … like building a house out of sticks and thinking it will last forever.

# PROVOCATIVE STATEMENT

A provocative statement is an opinion specifically meant to upset the listener and reader. It calls forth a strong reaction so they have to go on to the end. Maybe this would work:

> The three little pigs were turned out of their home and nothing could change that.

Here we're telling the listener about the horrible thing that happened to the little pigs, and it can't be undone no matter how much one might wish it. This next opening sentence might be even more provocative:

> Pigs are stupid and nothing you say will make me think otherwise.

# MIDDLE OF THE ACTION

The best way to involve the reader and listener of our stories is to cut out introductory and backstory material and begin with an action

when something has changed for the characters that compels the story forward, like:

> "I'll remember you always," the old sow called to her little pigs as she waved goodbye.

Or from the one of the pig's point of view:

> "You mean I can't live with you forever?" cried the littlest pig.

Both of these sentences plunge you into the drama of the story.

## CONFLICT

Just as it's good to start a story in the middle of the action, it's even better to quickly show the conflict.

> The three little pigs begged their mother, "Don't make us leave."

Or:

> "I can't keep you here," Mother said to her three little pigs, "and that's that!"

## SCRAPBOOK

This could also be a newspaper article, a journal entry, or a letter. For the three little pigs' scrapbook, I might have pictures of them as newborns, as young babies playing outside their house, blowing out birthday candles, and then waving good-bye to Mother. Then the words start with what happens to them after they set out on their own. The scrapbook is a great way to show backstory without writing anything.

A newspaper article might open with the headline:

> HUNGRY WOLF ON THE PROWL

A journal entry might be:

> October 1st. Today is the day Mother sent us away to find our fortunes.

A letter might begin:

Dear Mother,

We thought you'd like to know how we've been faring since we last saw you.

There you have it. Nine different ways to focus your first line.

Thinking *and* taking risks that are outside the box of your story will present all kinds of new directions for your writing. Play around with possible approaches for your first line, as you did experimenting with different voices to tell your story.

## WHAT'S NEXT?

In the following chapter we'll consider basic plotting techniques and ways to pump up the sagging middle of a story.

## BEFORE YOU GO ON

1. Look at your first line. Is it the best it can be? Experiment, changing it according to the eight different ways of focusing in this chapter.

    a. Time
    b. Mood
    c. Setting
    d. Opinion
    e. Provocative statement
    f. Middle of the action
    g. Conflict
    h. Scrapbook

2. Look at the first lines in your published books. Do they grab you or not? Why?

3. Some writers find it a great story sparker to make up first lines. Free-associate for a few minutes and jot down some intriguing ones. Then pick a favorite and write a story from it.

4. Are you still having trouble revising your opening to your complete satisfaction? Perhaps you are like Blaise Pascal who said, "That last thing one discovers in writing a book is what to put first." If this is you, don't be discouraged. Set your opening aside and continue on with the exercises in this book. Then come back to it with a fresh mind.

5. Read a new picture book.

# CHAPTER 9

# THREE-ACT STRUCTURE AND BASIC PLOTTING

 *A plot is what happens when there is a problem that needs solving.* —Jean E. Karl

Are you like me when it comes to plotting?

I have a great idea for an opening. It's catchy, the character is appealing, and the problem involving. I've cut away the setup and started smack in the middle of the action. Often I know how the book is going to end. And that ending is tight and satisfying.

The problem is I don't know how to get to my ending in a way that isn't:

1. too thin to fill up the middle of my book.
2. predictable and obvious from the get-go.
3. boring, oh so boring, even I yawn while I'm writing it.
4. lacking in tension and incentives for the reader to turn the page.

My story frequently has a beginning and an end, but didn't have anything in the middle.

When books fail, the author is usually driving along a word highway without a map to show the way to the destination.

Whether you've been lost on a real road, as I was in Italy years ago in the middle of the night with no idea where I was or where I was going, or simply lost in your story, it's scary.

This chapter is about how to drive your story forward. But a word of caution: No one map can get *every* story to its destination. Each story reaches its end sometimes traveling down roads similar to the roads of other stories, but most often demanding its own path. Much as we'd love a simple formula to plug every story into, it makes writing much more challenging not to have one. It also makes every working day a challenge and, therefore, stimulating.

Nevertheless, understanding and putting into practice basic plot structure will strengthen your writing and decrease the frustration of eash story journey.

The plot structure we use today did not develop full-blown overnight. It has evolved over centuries of writing and storytelling. No one says every story must be written within this framework, but most authors find it to be the most dramatic way of writing.

# THREE-ACT STRUCTURE

Three-act structure simply means having a beginning, middle, and end. John Gardner states it this way: "In nearly all good fiction, the basic—all but inescapable—plot form is: A central character wants something, goes after it despite opposition (perhaps including his own doubts), and so arrives at a win, lose, or draw."

How might these three parts be constructed in our picture books?

The opening is the first act. The characters and problem are introduced, along with an inciting incident, or turning point, that moves the reader from Act I to Act II. This first act in picture books needs to come smack at the beginning—certainly within the first half-page of your typed manuscript. It's a brief act that forces you quickly into Act II.

In Act II, the main character takes action, and more action, and even more action to solve his problem. The act most often culminates in a low moment when all feels lost.

Then it's time to move to our short and final Act III.

The last act contains the resolution of the problem, or the ending. Once the problem set out in the beginning of the picture book is solved, the story is over, finished—except perhaps for quickly tying up any loose ends. The solution of the problem usually occurs on pages 30 and 31 of a published picture book. The tying together of any dangling threads falls on page 32.

The acts in picture books, unlike acts in a play, are not equal in length. A drawing might look like this.

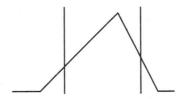

The left-hand vertical line indicates the end of Act I. The other vertical line indicates the end of Act II. As you can see by this visual picture, the first and third acts are brief. This three-act structure is just as valid for nonfiction and concept books as for fiction. In non-fiction, the first act is where the subject is introduced. In the second act, the subject is explored and expanded upon. In the final third act, the writer comes to a conclusion.

Concept books are the same. The first act introduces an idea, then expands on that in the second act and wraps everything up in the third act.

The second act most often needs work. Many manuscripts fail in the middle of the book.

So you can see how this three-act structure works, let's make up a story about a boy named Steve.

> Act I: Steve lives in a small town where everyone knows everyone and it's safe for him to walk to the store by himself. Today he wants to buy a comic book.
>
> Act II: He takes the money he's saved out of his piggy bank and goes to the store.
>
> Act III. He buys his comic book.

That's the end.
    Does this work?
    No!
    Why not?

Steve wants to buy a comic book and he does. There's no tension. It's too easy. The only action consists of walking to the store and choosing a comic. Nothing stops him. Nothing interferes with his goal. This story is seriously missing a second act. But it's also missing something else.

What happens if we up the stakes for Steve? Suppose instead of going to buy a comic book, today is his mother's birthday and he wants to get her a present. Now we've put added weight onto his purchase. It's not for him. It's for his mom's special day.

But if Steve opens the piggy bank, gets the money, goes to the store and buys a bar of her favorite soap, the story is still too easy. There's no problem and ... **no problem means no tension.**

No tension means bored readers and, worse yet, a rejection from an editor.

How can we add tension?

Suppose Steve opens his piggy bank and finds it empty. Now we have a real problem. Steve knew he had money. Where is it? How can he buy something for his mom without money? Steve looks under his bed and *Wow* There's his five-dollar bill. He's saved.

Is this a good story?

Not yet. It's over way too quickly.

# THE RHYTHM OF THREES

Let's revise by adding three attempts of Steve to solve the problem.

> Steve opens his piggy bank and it's empty!
> First Steve looks under his bed.
> No money there.
> Next he looks in his desk.
> No money there.
> The third place he looks is in the cushions of his chair.
> Still no money.
> Steve plops down on the chair. He's sure he's never going to find the money to buy a present for his mother.

What happened here?

We gave the reader more time to get to know Steve and to feel his increasing tension. The reader is more connected to him and his problem. Now we worry for Steve.

This rhythm of threes is all around us.

Three strikes and you're out.

Father, Son, and Holy Ghost.

Goldilocks and the Three Bears.

The Three Little Pigs.

It's part of our history and our culture.

Why?

Because it's satisfying.

Three failures up the stakes so the reader worries more for the main character.

But Steve's story still lacks *interesting action*. All Steve does is look and look and look. Boring words and pictures! There's more to action than threes.

# VARIED ACTION

Sticking with Steve, let's suppose he finds the money in his piggy bank and starts off to the store.

> At the park, he stops to join his friends for a game of softball. In his first at bat, he hits a home run! Wow! Is he happy! But he remembers his mom's birthday present, waves good-bye to his friends, and goes on toward the store.
>
> On the way he offers to help his mother's friend Mrs. Binder, weed her garden.
>
> When that's finished, he pauses to chat with police officer Hurley, who afterward blows her whistle, holds up her hand, and stops the traffic so Steve can safely cross the street.
>
> Then Steve walks on to the store where he buys the soap. Then he goes back home to give his mother the present.

More action?

Of course.

Varied action?

Absolutely.

> Steve plays softball and scores a run.
> He helps Mrs. Binder in her garden.
> Then he talks to the police officer.

We have action here, but it's not the right kind of action.

The actions in this series are *incidental*. These things could happen in any order. Steve could garden with Mrs. Binder before he plays softball. Officer Hurley could stop traffic for him on the way home from the store.

The action we want in our stories is action that leads directly to a reaction, that leads to another action.

## CAUSE-AND-EFFECT ACTION

Because this is where many manuscripts fall flat, let's go back to Steve's story to understand the difference between incidental action and cause-and-effect action.

> Steve gets his money out of his piggy bank. He has just enough to buy his mom her favorite bar of soap. He leaves the house and passes the park where his friends yell, "Come on Steve! We need another player." He stops to join them in a game of softball.
>
> But this time, instead of scoring a run, Steve slams the ball through Mrs. Binder's window.
>
> CRASH!
>
> Everybody races away.
>
> Everyone but Steve. He's stunned. He can't move. Needless to say, Mrs. Binder finds him. Tears fill her eyes. She struggles to make do on her monthly social security check and replacing a broken window is not in her budget.
>
> Help!
>
> Steve shifts from one foot to the other. "I'm sorry," he says. But he can tell by her tears an apology won't be enough. "I'll pay for the window," he adds, and reaches deep into his pocket. He hands Mrs. Binder the six quarters, ten dimes, five nickels, and seventeen pennies he's saved for his mother's present.

Mrs. Binder counts the change. "Thank you, Steve," she says. "Two dollars and ninety-seven cents is a sweet gesture, but not nearly enough for my new window."

Thinking quickly, Steve offers to work for her. She accepts and together they sweep up the broken glass. Then he helps her weed her flower garden.

However, Steve is distracted the whole time, trying to figure out what he can do now for his mother's birthday present.

When they finish, since he has no money, Steve doesn't even bother going to the store. What's the point?

Dejectedly he starts home.

Poor Steve!

He's crying now. His eyes are so filled with tears and his mind so concerned about what to give his mother that he steps into the street without looking.

Uh-oh!

A car's coming down the road.

Double uh-oh!

The car is speeding!

Triple uh-oh!

The car is a *police* car!

Quadruple uh-oh!

SCREEEEEEEE-EEEEEECH!

Yikes! This is big trouble.

We mentioned earlier about the term *page turn* in writing picture books. This is your classic page turn. Don't you have to find out whether Steve gets hit by the police car?

I turn the page.

The police car stops just before it hits Steve. Thank heavens! BUT ...

Officer Hurley is both furious and frightened over what might have happened if she hadn't stopped in time. She gives Steve a talking to and then takes him home in the police car to tell his mother.

Now Steve has no present for his mother and, to make matters worse, he's going to be in trouble with her.
This is Steve's darkest moment.

I don't know about you, but I'm eager to see how the story ends.

Look closely at the cause-and-effect pattern of these actions. Steve is walking to the store to buy his mother a present. On his way he passes the park, his friends call to him, and he joins them. If he weren't going to the store, he wouldn't have been tempted to play softball. If he hadn't been playing softball, he wouldn't have broken Mrs. Binder's window. If he hadn't broken the window, he wouldn't have had to give her his money and work for her. If he hadn't been so upset by his new poverty, he wouldn't have crossed the street without looking and he wouldn't have almost gotten run over by Officer Hurley who now, at Steve's worst moment, is going to tell his mom how she almost hit him. Steve has no money, no present, and to make matters worse, everything he's done has led to the possibility of getting in huge trouble with his mom … on her BIRTHDAY!

I hope you noticed that using **cause-and-effect action,** we've still kept our **rhythm of threes.** *One,* playing baseball, leads to *two,* breaking a window, leads to *three,* almost getting killed. We've also made sure of something else here.

# ESCALATING ACTION

Notice that I didn't write the biggest, most exciting action first. In a humorous book, don't place your funniest incident first, either. Stories need to build from smaller to larger, as I did in Steve's story, or from slightly laughable to ridiculous in a humorous story.

Suppose Steve had almost gotten hit by the police car first and joined the baseball game at the end. The story wouldn't have been nearly as satisfying.

The three-act structure is critical to everything you write. Also important are **the rhythm of threes** to increase your tension, just as **cause-and-effect** and **escalating action** build toward your end.

For a classic example of this in a published book, look at *Ming Lo Moves the Mountain* by Arnold Lobel.

In the first two sentences, we learn that Ming Lo and his wife love their house at the bottom of a mountain, but they don't love the mountain. They decide to move the mountain. But how?

They resolve to ask the village wise man. We have the problem and the turning point, and that is the end of Act I.

In Act II, the first action suggested by the wise man is to cut down a large tree and push it against the mountain.

When that doesn't move the mountain, Ming Lo goes back to the wise man for another (his second) suggestion. This time the wise man says, "Take some pots and pans from your kitchen and pound them with spoons. Yell as loud as you can and frighten the mountain into moving." Notice how this suggestion is more ridiculous than the first.

Ming Lo and his wife try this approach and fail, too. Their frustration mounts and Ming Lo returns to the wise man whose third suggestion is to take cakes and breads to the spirit who lives at the top of the mountain. Because the spirit is always hungry, he will grant whatever they wish. Ming Lo and his wife do what they are told. You can probably guess the outcome: Ming Lo rushes back to the wise man.

Notice how one event causes another. Ming Lo and his wife want to move the mountain. Because they don't know how, they go to the wise man. He makes a suggestion. It doesn't work, so they go back again. This suggestion doesn't work, so they go back again. And his new suggestion doesn't work either.

We're up to three different tries to move the mountain. Now we think Ming Lo and his wife will have to endure the mountain's falling rocks and stones, and the holes caused by them in their home, forever.

This is the story's darkest point. And here we are propelled into Act III, where Ming Lo and his wife follow another suggestion from the wise man. They bundle up everything in their house and then bundle up the sticks the house was made out of. They carry some of the bundles on the tops of their heads. Others they carry in their arms. Then they face the mountain, close their eyes, and dance the dance the wise man taught Ming Lo.

Because the dance involves putting one foot behind the other, over and over again, when they open their eyes several hours later, the mountain is far away. Problem solved. In a short pulling together of loose ends, Ming Lo and his wife rebuild their house and put their belongings away. They live happily ever after. And that's the end of Act III.

In this story we have three acts, the rhythm of threes, one event leads to another, and each attempt to solve the problem becomes increasingly ridiculous. Arnold Lobel, who also did the illustrations, shows the wise man smoking a pipe. Each time Ming Lo returns, the puff of smoke around the wise man grows bigger and bigger to show his increased pondering before each new suggestion.

# TESTING A MANUSCRIPT

How do we determine whether a story has three acts?

First of all, I print out a hard copy of my manuscript. Then I use a colored highlighter to mark where the story problem catapults the reader into the second act. Afterwards I look for the place where the character solves the problem that was set up in the beginning. I highlight that with the same color. The in-between part is the second act.

On separate sticky notes, I write each time the character takes an action toward solving the problem. (I like brightly colored sticky notes. They make me smile and therefore my writing feels less tedious.) Are there at least three? If not, I must add more. If I have more than three, perhaps some can be deleted.

Then I spread the action notes on my desk or table to make sure each action leads directly to another. If so, on another note I draw an arrow that leads from one to the other and place it in between them. If they don't lead directly, I know I must rewrite so they do, or shift around the order of my actions.

Last of all, I consider whether my sticky notes build to an exciting climax. If the most dramatic action comes first, I need to rework and reshuffle. Then I pretend I'm playing cards and deal myself one story hand. The scenes aren't building. I don't like that hand? I shuffle them around again and try another order of events.

This test shows me exactly where my plotting is strong and where it needs extra work.

Once in a while after testing the manuscript where I've tried to use the **rhythm of threes, cause-and-effect**, and **escalating action, I'll discover that** something is still missing.

Raymond Chandler said, "When the plot flags, bring in a man with a gun."

Fortunately, we writers for children have several less violent methods to up the ante in our books.

## Working Toward a Goal or Event

A goal or an event ups the stakes and sets a time limit for how long the main character has to solve his problem. Perhaps a child is going to compete in a spelling bee and is studying hard to memorize the words. Or perhaps a baseball game is coming up and a girl needs to improve her hitting.

Our Steve has always worked toward the event of his mother's birthday and the goal of finding her a present.

In *How to Make an Apple Pie and See the World* by Marjorie Priceman, the main character wants to make an apple pie but doesn't have the ingredients. She travels the world to collect them and finally bakes her pie. She achieves her goal.

*Mary Veronica's Egg* by Mary Nethery is a story of working toward an event. Mary Veronica wants the creature inside her egg to come out quickly so it can win the Most Unusual Pet ribbon at her school pet fair on Friday. The days pass, and we become more and more nervous that the egg won't hatch. And in fact, in a nice twist, it doesn't hatch until it's too late to win for the ribbon.

## Rhythm of Sevens

Instead of trying to solve a problem three times, consider trying seven times. In the same way that the rhythm of threes is all around us, we also have the rhythm of sevens in our days of the week and *Snow White and the Seven Dwarfs*. It's familiar and comfortable and certainly forces the reader to wonder when in the world the character is going to solve his problem.

How might this rhythm of sevens work in our story about Steve?

First Steve looks in his piggy bank. It's empty.

Then he looks in his desk. No money there.

He looks in the cushions of his chair. Still no money.

Now Steve is desperate. He looks in the bathroom cabinet.

He looks in the dishwasher and behind the TV. He even looks in his father's shoes.

You can see how this can stretch a story. I think it works fine for Steve looking seven places, but when I try seven actions that happen to him on the way to the store, I'm not sure. What do you think?

Suppose (1) Steve gets the money out of the bank and starts to the store. (2) On the way to the store, he stops to play softball. (3) He hits Mrs. Binder's window and (4) has to stay and clean up the mess. (5) Mrs. Binder is so grateful, she takes him for ice cream, which means that (6) when Steve finally reaches the store, it's closed. But he sees someone inside. (7) He bangs and bangs on the door.

Maybe my problem is that the actions aren't so great. Each writer has to decide when enough is enough with his or her story.

Candace Fleming uses this rhythm of sevens when she retells a story by Benjamin Franklin in her charming *The Hatmaker's Sign*. The hatmaker is designing a sign for his shop. He goes through seven different combinations of words and pictures before he finally returns to the original sign.

Still feel like something's missing in your story?

## Suspense

Of course, every picture book needs suspense. The reader wants to worry if the main character can solve the problem. Without worry, the story is too predictable.

I tried to increase the suspense by putting Steve into deeper and deeper trouble until he's in a police car being driven home.

In *Do Like a Duck Does!* by Judy Hindley, the listener will worry if the "hairy-scary stranger" can convince Mother Duck he is truly a duck and therefore get close enough to eat all her ducklings.

Play around with your story to see how you might increase the suspense so neither the reader nor the listener knows what the outcome will be until the very end.

Just as I finally found my way back to our Italian hotel, keeping the three-act structure and basic plotting concepts in mind will help you arrive at the end of each new story.

## WHAT'S NEXT?

Picture books are short and focused and fortunately have the luxury of more techniques to organize and hold a story together. In chapter 10 we're going to see what those might be.

## BEFORE YOU GO ON

1. Test your own story in the manner covered here. Does your middle need to be expanded? If each action doesn't lead to the next, reshuffle your sticky notes. Perhaps you'll want to add some more actions and delete others. Rewrite if necessary.

2. Study your two published manuscripts. Mark their three acts. Then look at how they follow the techniques discussed in this chapter.

3. Rewrite a fairy tale or popular story like *Goldilocks and the Three Bears* or perhaps *Cinderella*, changing the characters or the setting but sticking close to the action. This is a great way to learn about plotting, and you'll experience how a well-written and enduring tale is plotted. Then you can apply it to your own writing.

4. Read a new picture book.

# HOLDING YOUR
# STORY TOGETHER

*The sinister thing about writing is that
it starts off seeming so easy and ends
up being so hard.* —L. Rust Hills

If only this quote weren't true.

But it is. Be that as it may, we picture book writers are lucky. We have eleven more wonderful techniques to help hold our stories together.

## DAYS OF THE WEEK

This is a fine way to organize your story. A good rule is if you aren't going to mention every day of the week, don't mention any. When you state a specific day, you set the reader up to expect the rest of them. Days of the week might work nicely for Steve's story.

> Suppose he overhears Dad talking on Sunday about Mother's birthday coming up the following Saturday.
>
> On Monday he opens his piggy bank and counts five nickels and seventeen pennies. What's he going to do? He needs more than two dollars to buy the soap.
>
> On Tuesday he offers to help Dad mow the lawn. Dad pays him two quarters.

That's still not enough for the soap, so on Wednesday at the park he crawls under the benches and picnic tables and lucky Steve finds two quarters and three dimes.

On Thursday he helps Mrs. Binder in her garden, and she pays him two quarters and five dimes.

On Friday, Steve's father gives him his allowance of two dimes.

Now Steve has enough money to go to the store on Saturday and buy his mother the soap.

Books including the days of the week are popular with teachers because they reinforce the learning of those days that goes on in preschool and kindergarten.

*I.Q. Goes to the Library* by Mary Ann Fraser is a fine example of a published book organized in this manner. It's Library Week, and on Monday the main character, a mouse named I.Q., goes to the library with the class whose room he lives in. Each day is a new adventure in the library until Friday, when he gets his own card and can check out a book. He doesn't mind being alone in the classroom on Saturday because he has his book to read. On Sunday he dreams of other books he can check out.

# A JOURNEY

Don't most of us love to take a trip? The anticipation, the packing, the actual trip, and the unusual adventures along the way. The goal of a journey is to reach the destination. Stories that take a reader on such a journey are very popular. Steve's story could be a journey *if* he made it all the way to the store and bought his mother the soap.

*Owen & Mzee: The True Story of a Remarkable Friendship* by Isabella Hatkoff, Craig Hatkoff, and Dr. Paula Kahumbu is a nonfiction book about a baby hippopotamus named Owen who was separated from his mother and their group of hippos during the tsunami in December 2004. He was rescued and taken to a new place to live, where he bonded with a 130-year-old tortoise named Mzee.

*The Buffalo Storm* by Katherine Applegate is the fictional story of a girl named Hallie and her family who join a wagon train to travel to Oregon.

# CIRCULAR FORM

This technique is connected to the one just mentioned. Here, instead of reaching the destination and stopping, the character returns to the place where he began. Or a writer might start at one point, say a park, and come back again to that same park. Steve's story could go from home to the store and back home again.

In Donald Hall's Caldecott Medal-winning *Ox-Cart Man*, the farmer loads up his cart with everything that his family had made, or grown, over the past year and goes into town, where he sells everything. Then he returns home to start the cycle of making and growing all over again.

A circular story might also begin with a certain phrase and end with that same phrase or a slight change of the wording of the initial phrase. It brings wonderful closure to a piece of writing. Tricia Gardella's *Just Like My Dad* opens with the phrase, "When I get up in the morning, I put on my cowboy hat, my chaps ... and my spurs ... just like my dad." Then the picture book follows the little boy and his dad through all the activities of a ranching day. At the end of the day, Dad is tucking the boy into bed and the boy says, "I never get tired of hearing him say that one day I will be a great cowhand ... just like *his* dad."

# COMPARISON

Suppose we compared the activities of Steve and his father.

> Steve opens his piggy bank.
> Father opens his wallet.
> Steve finds $2.97.
> Father finds a twenty-dollar bill.
> Steve walks to the store.
> Father's not very nice and drives to the store alone.
> Steve buys his mother soap.
> Father buys his wife a book.

Not a very interesting story, but you get the idea of how this might work. Usually the two come together at the end. Perhaps the last scene would be at the birthday party when Steve and Father give Mother their presents and she kisses them both.

But there's another problem here. It's the comparison between Father and Steve. In picture books, try to get rid of adults as much as possible, or as one of my former teachers Terry Dunahoo used to say, "Kill the parents." Let's see what happens if we kill Steve's father and instead give Steve a sister named Sarah.

> Steve opens his piggy bank.
> His older sister Sarah opens her purse.
> Steve finds $2.97.
> Sarah finds $3.15. "I have more money than you do."
> Steve says, "I don't care!" and leaves the house.
> Sarah says, "You do too care. I can buy Mother a better present than you can."
> Steve shuffles to the store.
> Sarah skips past Steve.
> At the store, Steve looks at the soaps.
> Sarah looks at the perfumes.

You get the idea.

Doesn't it feel more connected to children when the two characters are children? I might end this by somehow bringing the two to a point where they decide to pool their money and buy something extra nice for Mother together.

I need to pause here and admit that none of these stories would probably make a great book in their present forms. These rough outlines of stories are meant only to illustrate the concepts and get you thinking of ways you might plot and strengthen your middles.

To see a published book written as a comparison, read *Outside, Inside* by Carolyn Crimi. It is about to rain outside, and the story moves back and forth between the storm and the girl and her cat inside. At the end, the rain stops and the main character opens the door and the inside and outside meet.

# ALPHABET

This is often used by nonfiction writers to organize their information. My book *Eight Hands Round: A Patchwork Alphabet* introduces a different patchwork design name for each letter. Michelle Markel uses the alphabet in her book *Cornhusk, Silk, and Wishbones: A Book of Dolls From Around the World* to introduce children to unusual dolls. The photographs are stunning.

However, if you're writing fiction, more and more publishers want the alphabet organization to also tell a story. It's not enough these days to just list *A is for Apple, B for Banana.*

I'm getting tired of writing about Steve all the time. I want to write about his sister Sarah for a while.

But wait!

I can't change my main character midstory, and you shouldn't either. Your main character needs to come on first and leave last ... so Steve will have to continue as the main character throughout this chapter.

> Steve decides to pick up things around the house and yard and put them in a bag for his mother's birthday. He finds an Acorn in the yard, then a Bird's feather. He picks a Cherry off the tree, and on and on. Remember that collecting things isn't enough—we need a problem. Perhaps Steve can't find something that begins with Z or make it earlier with K or Q. We also need the letters to be connected in some general way. Perhaps Mother loves nature so he chooses everything outside. It also makes a stronger book when a letter is connected to the one that follows or went before. Perhaps the Acorn is next to the Bird's feather and while Steve leans over to pick them up, the Cherry falls off the tree and bops him on the head. OW!

One word of warning! An alphabet book needs to use *every* letter of the alphabet. You can't cheat by using a hard *C* sound for *K*. But you can be creative with your letters. In my book *Everything to Spend the Night*, I had trouble coming up the letter *X* until I thought about how the little girl might bring her game of jacks. The shape of jacks have always made me think of the letter *X* so I wrote, "I brought my jacks. Toss the *X*s."

June Sobel, in *B is for Bulldozer: A Construction ABC*, uses words related to construction, but the mystery of the final project only unfolds partially in the illustrations around the letter *W*. It is not until the letter *Z* (*Zoom!*) that we see the workers have built a roller coaster.

Alphabet storybooks are popular with teachers because they reinforce their students' learning of the alphabet.

# COUNTING

Teachers also look for counting books, but as with alphabet books, number books must tell a story.

Rethinking Steve, let's say he decides to give Mother one acorn, two bird feathers, three pinecones, etc. The problem is this story doesn't build. It's just routine counting. How could I build and bring some tension to it?

Suppose Steve's bag breaks? Or suppose he can't find ten and then it turns out to be something right under his nose, like ten pebbles? Remember: Story, story, story! That's what we're trying to create in our picture books for children.

In my book *Count on Culebra,* the snake Culebra counts from one to ten in Spanish. To distract Iguana from her sore toe, he orders his friends to attach objects such as *un* rolling pin, *dos* kettles, *tres* skillets. onto the rope tied on her tail.

In *Hippity Hop, Frog on Top*, Natasha Wing tells of frogs climbing on top of one another to learn what's on the other side of the wall. It takes ten of them to finally see an alligator! Then, "Hippity-hop, frogs ker-plop."

# REPETITIVE PHRASE

A phrase that's repeated in a story adds rhythm and poetry. It can also be used to indicate the passage of time for younger readers who don't understand the concepts of tomorrow, next week, or next year.

What repetitive phrase could I use for Steve? Perhaps he wanted to get his mother that bar of soap more than anything. I'd repeat, "Mother will really like my soap" several times, not too many, to raise the tension and emphasize the point.

Kids love hearing repetitive phrases. They anticipate them and say them along with the adult. They feel like they're "reading." But too often, beginning writers overuse these phrases. When you're starting out, a good rule of thumb is *less is better.* Or you might consider varying the phrase here and there so it isn't predictable.

My favorite book using a repetitive phrase is Susan Fletcher's *Dadblamed Union Army Cow.* During the Civil War, a young man went off to join the Union Army and his cow, or as he calls her, "That dadblamed cow," followed him to the enlistment office, and to the railway station, and onto the train … and all the way to the war. All sorts of troubles ensue, so she varies the young man's phrase to "a dadblamed heavy cow," and later, "a dadblamed dangerous cow," and finally, happily "a dadblamed hero."

# MONTHS OF THE YEAR

I'm not sure months of the year would work for Steve's story. Would a child today think about what to give his mother for her birthday for one long year?

Maybe, though, I could move Steve back to colonial times. Life was slower and more leisurely then. I might pick a name more popular back then, like Miles. (For now, let's glide over the fact that in colonial times, birthdays were not the big deal they are today.)

> Miles is upset because in January he doesn't have anything for his mother's birthday. Miles decides next year will be different. He will carve Mother a duck. She loves ducks. He whispers his secret to his sister.
>
> All February, it is too cold and snowy to go out and find wood for the carving, so he imagines the duck he'll make her. Should his duck be sitting, standing, or perhaps in flight?
>
> When March comes, Miles goes out on the first sunny day to search for the perfect piece of wood. He searches and searches.
>
> In April, he finally finds an ideal one. Unfortunately, it's wet from the spring rains and he has to wait until May for it to dry.

And on and on and on. It might not turn into a very good story, but playing around, even if you never use the new form, is never wasted time. It allows you to envision your story in all its myriad possibilities.

Karen Winnick, in *A Year Goes Round: Poems for the Months*, organizes her lovely poems by the months. For example, March poems are titled "Wind" and "Quiet Morning." September's poems are "Summer's End" and "Dodge Ball."

# SEASONS

This is easier to use than months of the year. It doesn't work for me with Steve's story for the very same reason that kids of today probably wouldn't spend that much time thinking about a present, but it could work if I change Steve into a bear. Bears live according to the seasons. Let's call Steve Little Cub and meet him in winter, snuggled close to his mother. It's cold and he's hungry. He dreams of honey. When he finally goes out in spring, he vows he and his mother will never again be hungry in winter. To accomplish this, he decides to bring a beehive into their den. He can't find one in March, April, or May, so in the summer he builds one. In the fall, he has to attract the bees so they'll come make the honey. Of course, for this story to be successful, I would need to do a great amount of research on bees and when and how they make their honey, but it's a story possibility to consider.

I used this technique with my nonfiction book *The Seasons Sewn: A Year in Patchwork*. Because people's lives in pioneer times were closely tied to, and dependent on, the seasons, it was a natural way to organize the patchwork patterns. Gail Gibbons, in *The Seasons of Arnold's Apple Tree*, does exactly what the title says—captures the changes on a tree throughout the year.

# STORY WITHIN A STORY

Most often, an adult relates the story to a child. Suppose Father tells Steve about the time he got to ride in a patrol car and how terrified he was. You can see that this might take your story in a completely new direction.

I'd like to pause here again. I can't say this enough: Don't be afraid of new directions. Risk taking your story off the beaten track. You may discover it is exactly the thing to make your story jump out of the slush pile and onto the contract table.

A classic example of a story within a story is the sensitive and tender *Knots on a Counting Rope* by Bill Martin Jr. and John Archambault. Grandfather is telling a young boy the story of his birth. The boy, of course, has heard the story many times before and can almost tell the story himself. But this retelling reinforces the boy's knowledge of his strengths and his ability to survive no matter what.

## QUESTION AND ANSWER

Suppose we use this last technique with Steve's story. It might read like this:

> Will Steve have enough money to buy a present for his mother?
> No. There's no money in his piggy bank.
> Will Steve find money under his bed?
> No.
> Will Steve find money in his desk?
> No.

And on and on.

*Not a Box*, written and illustrated by Antoinette Portis, uses the question-and-answer format. An outside character we never see asks, "Why are you sitting in a box?" The young rabbit answers, "It's not a box." Because Antoinette is also the illustrator, she did not have to write, "It's a race car." She showed the picture of the bunny inside his black line box with his imagination of a speeding car colored in red around the box.

Feel free to use more than one of these techniques to strengthen your middle. In *Mañana, Iguana*, I used the three-act structure, cause and effect, and also escalating action where Iguana gets more and more frustrated that her friends won't help her prepare for their fiesta. For extra punch, the characters are working toward an event, a fiesta to celebrate spring.

Then for good measure I added not one, but several, repetitive phrases: "Mañana, Iguana," "Yo no!," and "And she did."

And last but not least, the story followed the days of the week.

After you write your story with the three-act structure using the rhythm of threes, cause-and-effect action, and escalating action, take time to experiment with these eleven techniques to add depth and structure to your drive from the beginning to the end of all your stories.

Easy, right? Of course not.

When you're alone with your story, it's tough and challenging.

Unfortunately in each story you will have to use different techniques to reach the destination of everything you write.

That's the challenge of writing *and* that's also what keeps writing stimulating. When you're working on a story and you suspect that it's not moving forward, or maybe it even comes to a dead stop, **trust your intuition**. You may be missing an act. Perhaps your action isn't cause and effect and escalating. Perhaps you need to use one or more of the techniques discussed here. Experiment with them. Maybe one will help you reach your goal—a published book!

## WHAT'S NEXT?

We've made it through the middle of picture books. Now it's time to make sure your ending is as satisfying as your opening and your middle.

## BEFORE YOU GO ON

1. Check your manuscript to see if you use one of the techniques discussed. Some stories incorporate several. Play around by adding one or two, or changing the techniques to improve your story.

2. Reread your two published manuscripts to see what techniques, if any, the authors used in the middle.

3. Read a new picture book.

# DOES YOUR STORY MAKE IT TO THE END?

*A book should end with the*
*unexpected expected.* —*Jane Yolen*

A book without a strong ending feels like dinner without dessert. Something is lacking. In the same way chocolate cake can leave one feeling full and satisfied, a great ending can leave one pleased and contented. And in the same way chocolate cake is so tasty you want more, even though you know you shouldn't indulge, a good ending compels a reader to go back and read the story again … and again …and again. That taste of chocolate and those final words linger in the mind long afterwards.

On the other hand, a weak ending leaves an unpleasant taste in one's mouth. Far too many books start with great promise only to fall flat. It's too bad the third act in any book, play or, movie has such power to make us either love, be ambivalent, or even hate everything that went before.

Some writers, like Katherine Anne Porter, feel: "If I didn't know the ending of a story, I wouldn't begin. I always write my last line, my last paragraphs, my last page first."

Other writers don't have any idea where the story will take them and insist on being surprised by what comes out of their mind, via their fingers, onto the computer screen. They let the characters lead.

Regardless of when you write your ending, labor long and hard to avoid giving a blah feeling to your reader and listener. Here are some points to consider in evaluating your ending.

## THE ENDING MUST NOT BE PREDICTABLE

It needs to originate from the story yet still be surprising. Who wants to read any farther along in a mystery if we know immediately the butler killed the master of the house? Who wants to read more in a picture book if we are certain how the bully will get his comeuppance? Naturally, we want to assume the bully will be brought down, but we don't want to know *how* that will happen until the end.

## THE ENDING MUST SOLVE THE PRESENTING PROBLEM

Sometimes writers start out with one problem, introduce another problem along the way, and the ending solves only that second problem. Suppose the main character is terrified of the neighbor's dog, who leaps and barks and growls whenever he passes the gate. That's the presenting problem. But one day he and his big brother walk a different way to avoid the dog. When they come to the corner, the main character is too frightened to cross the street. He worries a big truck might rumble down the road. Will it be able to stop? He overcomes that fear by grasping his brother's hand. Together they look and listen for oncoming traffic. Then they cross the street. And the author ends the story.

But what happened to the boy's fear of the neighbor's dog?

That still exists.

We've talked earlier about the importance of focusing one's story. You can understand how this focus helps create a satisfying ending.

## EVERYTHING YOU'VE WRITTEN RELATES TO THAT ENDING

If it doesn't, get out your pen or hit your delete key. Get rid of anything that doesn't move your story ahead. Sometimes, unfortunately, this will mean saying good-bye to your favorite words or lines.

Be brutal. If it's too painful, create a file of phrases you particularly love. Perhaps you'll be able to use them in a poem or another story.

# THE MAIN CHARACTER SOLVES THE PROBLEM

Too often in writing for children, a wise and well-meaning adult steps in to show the way. Get rid of that adult. We've talked earlier about empowering children, but the ending is the place where writers often forget to do that.

A child is bothered by a bully on the way to school. He tries several ways to stop this bully. They all fail so he asks Father for advice, and Father tells him what to do.

No! No! No!

The main character must come up with his own satisfying solution.

# THE MAIN CHARACTER CHANGES IN SOME WAY

Malcolm Cowley said, "Any fiction should be a story. In any story there are three elements: persons, a situation, and the fact that in the end something has changed. If nothing has changed, it isn't a story."

Therefore, the character in our picture books must learn something new about herself or her outlook on the world, or she has to overcome something within her that kept her from acting.

In a few stories a character struggles to change, or to effect some action, but cannot. Think about a child of divorced parents who tries over and over to bring them back together. Suppose by the end of the story he doesn't succeed but does recognize that nothing he can do will ever change the situation. Therefore he comes to accept that his parents' marriage is over. That acceptance is change.

# NO LUCKY COINCIDENCES INFLUENCE THE OUTCOME

A child doesn't want to go to school. He's afraid he'll flunk the spelling quiz. He begs Mother to let him stay home, but she is unmoved. He sobs. He feigns a stomachache. But nothing works, so he starts off to school, discouraged and dejected. All of a sudden (many editors and writers say *all of a sudden* should be banned in every story), as he passes a construction site, a bucket of paint falls on his head. It knocks him out and the workmen call an ambulance to take him to the hospital. He is kept for a twenty-four-hour observation.

Wow! Lucky him! He didn't have to take the spelling quiz after all. It's a happy ending for him, except for that scary time in the hospital, but is it satisfying to the listener?

Not at all.

## NO EXTRA CHARACTERS MATERIALIZE TO AID IN THE RESOLUTION

Suppose Coyote is about to attack Rabbit. His jaws are open. His mouth drools. Rabbit is sure she's a goner. But, just in time (you should probably eliminated *just in time* from stories, too), a hunter comes into the clearing, shoots Coyote, and saves Rabbit.

Again, a triple No! No! No!

What if Rabbit had a plan? She waited and waited until Coyote came so close he was eye to eye with her? Then Rabbit leaps over Coyote, sending him sprawling onto the ground. Rabbit escapes because of her own courage and smart thinking. She did it by herself. Bravo! We can enthusiastically cheer for her.

## ALL CHARACTERS PLAY AN IMPORTANT PART IN THE STORY

In picture books, unlike other books, we don't want characters to appear briefly only to disappear forever. Listeners will wonder what happened to the bully bothering the child on the way to school. They will anticipate that the best friend who went next door will come back. And they definitely will worry about the kitten who the main character fed milk to the night before, if it doesn't return. If characters like the ones in these examples merely make cameos, they can probably be cut. Notice I said *probably*. Exceptions to this do sometimes appear, especially in folk tales, where the main character is given powers along the way to help her on her quest. However, if those gifts are not part of the solution, the characters who gave them must go.

# THE ENDING COMES AT THE END OF THE BOOK

This point might seem obvious, but surprisingly it isn't.

In picture books, the solution to the presenting problem usually falls somewhere around pages 28 and 29, or better yet around pages 30 and 31 of the published book. But some writers solve the presenting problem in the middle and then go on and on and on. An example of this would be a story where the main character is working hard to improve her baseball skills for the championship game. She goes to the batting cages every day and hits and hits and hits. Then the big game comes, and her practice pays off. She smacks a home run that wins the game. Bravo!

But the writer isn't done yet. He tells us how the fans lifted her onto their shoulders, how they paraded her around the town and took her out for a celebratory dinner. He also shares an article praising her hit in the next day's paper. Enough already!

We were thrilled that she hit the home run. We don't need much more. Having the fans cheer and lift her up on their shoulders is plenty.

As Igor Stravinsky said, "Too many pieces finish long after the end."

When the problem is solved, your story is basically over, except for one last bit.

# LOOSE ENDS ARE TIED TOGETHER

Picture books have space on page 32 that's perfect for dealing with any unresolved issues. It's a page with room for a half-spread illustration (an illustration that doesn't cross over onto the next page). On page 32, there is no next page (unless the book is forty or more pages long). It is just right for a quick, sharp line. In Maurice Sendak's *Where the Wild Things Are*, Max has misbehaved and is sent to his room without his dinner. When he returns from his adventures with the Wild Things, lo and behold, his food is there and on page 32 we learn it's even warm and ready to eat. That last page is so satisfying it lingers in our memories long after we've closed the book.

Marjorie Priceman's last line of *How to Make an Apple Pie and See the World* works just as well. After a child discovers the market is closed and takes a worldwide trip to gather the ingredients to make an apple pie, she finally sits down with friends to eat the pie and discovers she has no

ice cream. She goes to the market and it's closed again. The reader fully expects another journey, but that is not what she gets. Check out this book to discover the pleasant surprise.

A successful last line brings a smile to the listener's face and a happy "Ah ha!" to her mouth. It states the unexpected, which on closer examination, turns out to be an "expected unexpected." It should make everyone want to read the book again.

In my book *Little Monkey Says Good Night,* Little Monkey has romped through the circus saying his good nights to everyone. He should be done, but he insists he has one more "good night" to offer. On page 32 we see him tucked into bed and hear him say, "Good Night, Me."

Because of the last line's importance, don't be lazy. Work hard shaping this final bit of your story.

In your ending, you want to leave no missing pieces, no string untied. While writers may leave some things up in the air in books for adults and older children, our young listeners don't want anything left untold as one might in a series of books.

Picture books are not series books in the traditional sense, even though we often have several books written about popular characters. *Olivia* is one example. *Rotten Ralph* is another. But each of these books can stand alone. They don't follow an unfinished thread from one book to another. Each picture book should exist on its own merits.

If a book is successful and an editor wants another, wonderful! That's like getting two scoops of ice cream instead of one for your chocolate cake. But don't start a series by leaving loose ends. Start a series by writing a runaway, best-selling book.

## DELETE ANY MORAL OR MESSAGE

Samuel Goldwyn once said, "If you want to send a message, use Western Union." Although he was talking to screenwriters, his advice also applies to picture book authors. Unfortunately a few writers forget that our stories should entertain. They should take the reader and listener to another place, another life, another world. If the writer wants to teach a lesson, she should write a nonfiction book or perhaps a book for the religious market. It won't hurt to restate that children have minds, just like adults. They will get the message without the author pounding them over the head with it.

While Aesop got away with tacking morals at the end of each of his stories, we don't do that anymore … unless we're writing a takeoff of Aesop's Fables as Arnold Lobel did in his Caldecott Medal-winning book *Fables*.

Today we write differently.

Think of the bad taste in one's mouth if, in the baseball story I mentioned earlier, the writer felt compelled to add a line about how the girl learned that practice and hard work pays off. The listener will get that lesson without it being explicity stated. Respect your audience.

## THE ENDING DOESN'T HAVE TO BE HAPPY, BUT IT MUST GIVE THE AUDIENCE HOPE

This hope is distinctive to picture books and to most writing for young children. Unlike adult books, where horrific things can happen and authors frequently share their depressed views of life, we children's authors try to write in an upbeat manner. There's too much war and death, too much hunger and cruelty, too many dangers for children to face in our world today.

Even the formerly simple and fun act of trick-or-treating has taken on ominous overtones. Adults can deal with worries and concerns better than young girls and boys. We owe it to today's children not to add to their anxieties.

This doesn't mean you can't write about war, death, or hunger. It's only to say that when you write about it, find something to give the listener a smidgen of hope.

Read *The Other Side* by Jacqueline Woodson, a sensitive story of two girls of different races tentatively reaching out to one another across a fence and forming a friendship. They still live in a racially separated world. But the ending indicates that maybe in the future things will improve.

Here are successful endings of three published books.

In *Three French Hens* by Margie Palatini, Phil Fox is down on his luck and decides to eat one of the fine French hens that appear at his doorstep on Christmas Eve. All does not go as he planned. The three

French hens pamper him so much he realizes he can't possibly eat them. For such kindnesses, he decides to give them the Christmas gifts they had put around his tree.

What a happy ending!

But they turn him down because they are Kosher chickens and don't celebrate Christmas. Isn't that a fabulous and unexpected twist? Phil Fox hugs them and together they celebrate the remaining twelve days of Christmas and the eight nights of Hanukkah.

Antoinette Portis's *Not a Box* has another charming ending. If you remember from our last chapter, an invisible speaker asks Bunny what he's doing with his box. Bunny repeatedly answers that it's not a box, it's something else he's conjured up in his imagination. His frustration grows and grows with each question until the speaker asks if it isn't a box, what is it?

The answer? It's my Not-a-Box.

In *Click, Clack, Moo: Cows That Type* by Doreen Cronin, the cows finally get the electric blankets they wanted and some for the hens, too. That should be the end, but no. The next morning a new note arrives from Duck, who had been carrying messages back and forth between Farmer Brown and the cows. It says the ducks want a diving board for their pond. Doreen Cronin solved the cows' problem and, in a fun twist, gave the ducks something, too.

I'm sure you can find many more examples of strong endings.

## WHAT'S NEXT?

Give yourself a pat on the back. You've finished every section on the structure of your story. In the following chapters we're going to move on to language and how to write in a lively and compelling manner.

## BEFORE YOU GO ON

1. Highlight with any color the place where the solution to your presenting problem comes in your story. If it's too early, delete or tighten what follows.

2. Give yourself a star or a happy face for each of the characteristics discussed in the chapter that you have successfully included in your ending.

    a. The ending must not be predictable.
    b. The ending must solve the presenting problem.
    c. Everything you've written relates to the ending.
    d. The main character solves the problem.
    e. The main character changes in some way.
    f. No lucky coincidences influence the outcome.
    g. No extra characters are thrown in to aid in the resolution.
    h. All characters play an important part in the story.
    i. The ending comes at the end of the book.
    j. Loose ends are tied together.
    k. Delete any moral or message.
    l. The ending doesn't have to be happy, but it must give hope.

Are you satisfied with your ending or do you need to revise?

3. Look at the endings of your published manuscripts in relation to the list above.
    Do they work? Why?

4. Read a new picture book.

LANGUAGE OF YOUR STORY

# TWO Ss OF STRONG WRITING

*Effective writing depends on showing through action, dialogue, or detail.* —*Olga Litowinsky*

Isn't it a relief to be done with picture book form? Now we'll turn to the two Ss of strong writing no matter if your audience is 1 or 101 years old. The first S is *Scenes.* The second S is *Show, don't tell.*

## SCENES

Nancy Lamb, in her wonderful book *The Writer's Guide to Crafting Stories for Children* says, "Think of scenes … as stepping stones that steer you down the path of your plot."

Too often, writers don't write the most important scenes. It's much easier to write, "The two friends made up" than to write the dialogue that allows the reader to see their feelings move from hostility to understanding.

Skipping an important scene is not only lazy writing, it is poor writing. Scenes are critical. They permit the readers and listeners to experience events with the character, watching the story unfold along with him. But to write a scene, you have to know what a scene is.

My favorite definition comes from Jack Bickham in his book *Scene and Structure.* He says scene is "a segment of story *action,* written *moment by moment without summary,* presented onstage in the story

'Now.' It is not something that goes on inside a character's head. It is *physical*. It could be put on the theater stage and acted out."

In those crucial italicized words, *action* means something is happening that you can see. A character punching another character is action. A character crying is action, and a character storming out of a room is more action. Because action is illustratable and contemplation isn't, we picture book writers must put as much action as possible into our manuscripts.

A scene is written *moment by moment without summary*. We see it exactly as it happened. It is not a condensation of an event.

A scene is *physical* in that it can be observed by outsiders.

## Why Write in Scenes?

Scenes are the best way to deliver conflict and tension. They are the primary device for making your readers and listeners respond the way you want them to. A scene allows them to play out in their minds what is taking place on the page. It takes your audience into the words, makes them all participants in your book, and helps control what they get from your words. The more vague you are, and the more you summarize, the more you pull your audience away from the character. You permit them to imagine what the scene might have been, and that can be very different from what you know happened.

## When Should You Write in Scenes?

A scene must do one of two things: either *advance the plot* or *reveal something new about your characters*.

If you have a scene in your picture book that doesn't move your story forward, write it as a narrative summary. For example, if the route your character takes to the soccer game isn't relevant, you can simply write, "When he arrived at the stadium." If your writing doesn't let the reader discover some unknown facet of your character, you can summarize this, too. But be sure your choice of scene or summary is the right one and you don't write a summary because the other is too challenging to write.

# How Do You Write a Scene?

Scenes are not easy—otherwise, everyone would be writing them. The important point is to throw your reader and listener into the action. They must be there every minute.

The best way for your audience to experience the scene is for YOU to put yourself in it. This isn't as difficult as it sounds. Be an actor. Pretend you are the character. Slip out of your skin and put on your character's skin. By this point, you've already done your character study. You know your character inside and out. In fact, you know your character so well you don't have to wonder what she might say; it's already on the tip of your tongue. Now pace the room like your character might, or fidget nervously in your chair. Speak in whispers, speak in shouts.

Don't be embarrassed or self-conscious. Unlike an actor on stage, no one has to see you. Each time you perform and revise, you refine and improve your performance.

Being a character used to scare me. When my critique group said, "You're not in the scene," I was sure I *never* could be in the scene. But with practice, I was surprised by how effortless it became. Soon it was second nature to me.

Try this simple exercise right now if you're afraid you can't become your character. Pretend you are a toddler coming into the room where you're reading this book.

What do you see?

I'll bet you notice things like the underside of a table. Maybe you can't see out of the window without pulling a chair over. You can't reach the top bookshelf or maybe even half of the bookshelves. The lamp bulb is too bright to look at. Toddlers touch everything. Is the rug smooth, thick, or bumpy?

Now be a different actor. Make believe you are an adult with a walker. What do you notice in the room? Is there a chair in the way that needs to be shoved to the side? What about an area rug? Might you worry about tripping? Is there a place you can put your walker while you sit on the sofa? Can you hear the hum of the air conditioner? Can you smell the chocolate cake baking in the next room?

Next pretend you're a cat. What does a cat see? Perhaps you see a spider hanging in the corner, the chair with the softest cushion, or the curtain's bright tassels.

Pretend you're in a hurry and can't find your car keys. Pretend, pretend, pretend, using all of your senses. The more you do, the less effort it will be to get into your character's skin and make scenes come alive for your listeners. I know authors who have gotten enormous help in their writing by taking acting classes. You might want to try it.

Having trouble writing a scene? Perhaps you need to go back and reread your character study. The better you know your characters, the easier it will be to slip into their skins.

Another reason your scene feels unsatisfying might be that you're writing too quickly. Writing a scene involves slowing down and paying close attention to each line. Pause to see what else might be happening around your character. Take as much time as you need to play with different possibilities of dialogue and action until you're sure you're writing what actually went on.

Slow! Slow! Slow!

Here are some words and phrases that warn you're not writing a scene:

> *Whenever* I walk past school …
> *Each time* the teacher calls on me …
> *Every time* Billy hits me …
> *Every day* I have to go to the grocery store …
> *Year after year* the leaves fall down …

These indicate that several scenes are being clumped together. If that's what you want, go ahead. But watch out that these clumpings are not scenes that should be played out individually on the page.

## Every Scene Has a Different Internal Rhythm

In the same way that life has different rhythms, our scenes must present different rhythms, too. We don't go along with the same emotional and psychological energy every hour of every day. Each twenty-four hours offers numerous and varied high and low points.

In strong, successful writing, the listener and reader should not only know intellectually what is happening, but also *feel it physically and emotionally.*

To understand this, imagine you are floating on your back in the warm waters of the Hawaiian Islands. You're riding the gentle ripples, enjoying the sun on your face, watching the clouds go by. Isn't it relaxing? Your body feels as light as a feather. Thoughts ramble through your mind, making connections that surprise you. You remember the last time you went swimming in the lake in Wisconsin. You remember your first kiss, sweet yet daring under the neighbor's porch. On and on you float with your old boyfriend's face smiling in the clouds.

Then ... you spot the telltale fin ... of a shark!

Your body tenses. Your mind races. One thought and one thought only: Am I going to die? Your breathing quickens. Your heart pounds. You're on heightened alert.

Notice what happened here. In the first example, you were relaxed. Your mind had time to contemplate and linger. The sentences were longer to match that lazy mood.

However, when the shark was spotted, everything changed. Sentences grew shorter, tighter. No time for metaphor or simile.

Your writing must echo the energy in the actions of each scene. We'll discuss how to do this in more detail in chapters 13 and 14.

Before we move on, let's make sure you understand the difference between a scene and a narrative summary. Here's another quiz. Write *S* if it's a scene and *N* if it's a narrative summary.

1. There was an accident on the way to the party.

2. Jon jumped up. "Let's go to the party."
   "Beat you there," Billy said, sticking his foot out and tripping Jon. "Sorry!" Billy smirked and dashed out of the house.
   Jon rubbed his knee. "I'll show him." He jumped up. "Ow!" He couldn't believe the pain. He hobbled down the street, cursing under his breath. "I hate Billy. I hate him."

3. "I just want to be your friend," she said between sobs. "That's all I want. Just like the old days."

4. She was upset to lose her friend.

5. Cat ignored Dog.

6. Dog wagged his tail.
   Cat leaped onto the chair. She licked her fur. She licked her paw.
   Dog put his snout onto the chair.
   Cat leaped onto the chair's soft back. She curled into a ball.
   Woof! Woof! barked Dog.
   Cat closed her eyes.

7. Lena paused at the fence. She gripped Mother's hand tightly.
   "Let's go home," she said.
   "But we just started walking," Mother said. "Come on."
   She tugged Lena's hand.
   Lena dug her heels into the grass. "No!" she cried. "A witch lives there. She wants to cook me for supper."

8. Lena didn't want to walk past the house.

Answers: 1. N 2. S 3. S 4. N 5. N 6. S 7. S 8. N

If you got them all right, you're on your way to understanding that oft-repeated phrase heard at conferences and in classes and our second *S*.

# SHOW, DON'T TELL

That phrase admonishes you to write a scene rather than a summary statement. However, *show, don't tell* applies not only to scenes, but also to descriptive phrases.

For example, the statement *Jeremy was happy* is a telling statement. *Jeremy's eyes lit up and a big smile stretched across his face* is specific. It allows the reader to come to the conclusion on her own that Jeremy was happy.

This is not insignificant. Imagine a sentence in a book that says *Henya was sad*. Now pretend we can't use the word *sad*. We have to describe the action that would make the reader realize she was sad. There are unlimited possibilities. Here are five:

1. Henya bit her lip. She turned away.
2. Tears streamed down Henya's cheeks.
3. Henya slumped in her seat.
4. Henya hurried into the closet and shut the door so she could be alone.
5. Henya busied herself making a peanut butter sandwich.

In number 1 we have a girl who tries to hide her upset, but we can tell it isn't easy so she has to turn away.

In number 2, Henya can't stop herself from showing strong emotion.

In number 3, the sadness shown is more subtle perhaps her feelings are less strong as the girl in number 2 or perhaps she just has better control over herself.

In number 4, Henya doesn't want anyone to see her sadness, so she rushes to the closet.

Number 5 is another subtle way to hide sadness, by busying oneself with another activity.

Each response indicates a different kind of character.

When you tell in a general statement, the reader must imagine what your character might do. Showing instead of telling makes *you, the writer,* define your character and paints a full picture for the reader and listeners of what is going on. It breathes life into the scene.

Every reader brings her own set of experiences and feelings about life to a book. If you tell instead of show, you give the reader too much power in creating your character.

Part of *show, don't tell* also concerns the details you choose for your story. Too many details will bog down the reader and slow the forward momentum of your story, but a specially placed vivid detail can be all the reader needs to be in the scene. Make sure the details in a picture book description are ones a child would understand.

For example: *The theater was huge* is a telling statement. Huge to whom? A mouse would find any theater huge, even if it only had one chair. Be specific. *The theater could seat one thousand patrons* is a clear explanation for an adult, but not so meaningful to our young listeners. *The theater was so big, from our seat in back, the actor on the stage looked as small as an ant* is much easier for a child to visualize.

David M. Schwartz, in his book *How Much Is a Million?*, explains everything in a manner children will comprehend. "If a goldfish bowl were big enough for a million goldfish … it would be large enough to hold a whale."

To make sure you understand this concept of *show, don't tell*, play around with changing the following ten telling statements into showing statements.

1. John was lonely.

2. There was an atmosphere of excitement and happiness.

3. The hole looked small.

4. There were too many cats and dogs.

5. Thoughts were spinning out of control in Sarah's mind.

6. He was physically and emotionally exhausted and also very excited about his trip.

7. Jessica kept swimming while people rushed to get out of the water.

8. Peter was scared.

9. At the Chicago Fair, people were awed by the sight of something completely new—a Ferris wheel.

10. He was worried the security patrol would stop him.

So you know you're on the right track, here are possible answers to compare with your own.

1. Jon looked longingly at the boys playing catch.

2. People around them started clapping and stomping. Susan nudged her date. "I can't wait for the show to start."

3. The hole looked smaller than my fist …

4. Cats sat on every windowsill. Dogs curled up all over the floor. While trying to reach the sofa I tripped over a two poodles and an English bulldog.

5. Should she tell the teacher? What will Billy think? Will her mom be mad? Sarah wished she could quiet the questions in her mind, but no. Will her sister tell on her first? Will Father be disappointed in her?

6. Ron flopped down on the bed. Exhausted from two hours of convincing his father he should be allowed to go to China with Matt, only half the battle was won. Now he had to get Mom to agree. He tossed and turned trying to come up with a plan that would work. When he couldn't stand the not knowing any longer, he took a deep breath. "Mom," he called.

7. The splashing all around Jessica was the first sign of trouble. A boy screamed. An old man bumped into her. "What's happening?" she asked. "Shark!" he yelled. That was all she needed to hear. She started swimming faster than she ever had before.

8. Peter trembled.

9. People stopped. They stared, leaning their heads back and shielding their eyes from the sun. An older man gasped. "I've never seen anything like it." A boy jumped up and down. "I want a ride. I want a ride."

10. Matt rubbed his sweaty hands against his jeans. He took a deep breath and tried to look normal as the security guard approached. "Hi." He waved casually, but he could feel his knees shaking.

How did you do here? Do you feel comfortable with the difference between showing and telling? Do you feel secure about writing scenes instead of summaries?

You've probably noticed that writing in scenes and showing instead of telling usually requires more words. Don't worry if writing in the two Ss initially adds extra words to a picture book manuscript you're trying to keep tight. Your story can be revised and written shorter. Showing doesn't have to increase your word count. *Cat was scared* can be shown by *Cat raced away* with. No additional words are used, but a vivid picture is drawn.

Many writers shy away from milking the conflict and sometimes skip completely over the dramatic turning point that leads to the climax. "They got into a huge fight" is less difficult to write than the scene showing the fight in all its gory details. But you must write that scene, however challenging it may be.

## WHAT'S NEXT?

We've covered two of the big general issues in writing. In chapter 13 we're going to get more specific about language and consider whether or not a story is best told in prose or poetry.

## BEFORE YOU GO ON

1. Look over your manuscript and circle places where you are writing a narrative summary rather than an unfolding scene. Also circle any places where you tell instead of show.

Do you have many? Good! That means you recognize where you need to work.

2. If you don't have many circles, let another writer go over your manuscript to make sure you spotted them all. In the beginning, it's often easier to pick these out from someone else's manuscript.

3. Now go back to all of those circles and write scenes rather than summary or write to show rather than tell.

4. Check your published manuscripts. Perhaps the ones you don't like did more telling than showing.

5. Read a new picture book.

# CHAPTER 13

# RHYME TIME

 *There is no better feeling to me than writing.
I love to make a picture come to life and
dance under my pen. —Lolita Prince*

This quote comes from a homeless woman active in the Los Angeles Downtown Women's Center writing workshop. When Lolita said, "I love *to make a picture come to life and dance under my pen,*" she expressed as good a definition of poetry as I know.

Poets use words, only words, to create pictures for the reader. The *dancing under the pen* relates to the music of those words. A successful poem not only brings up a visual image of the subject, but creates a physical reaction to enhance and reinforce the image through word choice and sounds, rhythm and rhyme.

Children love poetry. They love the music of it. They love to anticipate the rhyming words and say them with the adult. This is the beginning of their reading.

Many studies have shown that children who hear poetry from an early age become much better readers earlier than those not exposed to poems.

If this is true, why do editors so often groan when they read picture book manuscripts in rhyme? Why do they throw up their hands and say at conferences, "Please! No more rhymed picture books!"

The answer is simple. Most manuscripts fail when it comes to the elements of good poetry.

Yet writers persist. When they think of stories for children, they think of rhyme. It's lively. It's fun. And so they give it a try.

Why is it, I wonder, that people who have never studied poetry think they can write a poem? You wouldn't trust someone to perform surgery on you without having first studied medicine. You wouldn't let a pilot fly your plane if she hadn't taken flying lessons. And you wouldn't hire a teacher if he hadn't gone to college. But too many writers think they can write a rhymed picture book without any knowledge of poetry.

This chapter will help you determine whether you are capable of writing your story in rhyme or whether you need to educate yourself in poetry before you attempt it.

We're at that part of the book I warned you poetic phobics about earlier. Don't panic. Take a deep breath. Now take another deep breath. Believe me, I was a nervous wreck when I walked into my first poetry writing class. But I am here to attest that the study of poetry is the best thing I did to strengthen my ability to write publishable picture books.

So it's time to take a dip in the poetry pool. I guarantee that by reading the next two chapters and taking a few practice swims, you and poetry will get along just fine.

Let's get our feet wet with four elements of good poetry—*brevity, focus, consistent rhyme*, and *consistent rhythm*. These first two elements have already been discussed in relation to picture books. To help understand these concepts as they relate to poetry, we're going to use that well-known rhyme, *The Queen of Hearts*, by the prolific Mother Goose. Using this familiar poem will help you see the errors more clearly than you might pick them up in your own work.

# BREVITY

When I was in school and assigned to write papers of a certain length, I often padded my work. After all, I had to make the assigned word count.

Writing picture books, whether in poetry or in rhyme, forced me, and will force you, to unlearn your padding techniques. Picture books are short. Poems are short, too. Consider *The Queen of Hearts*:

> The Queen of Hearts she made some tarts,
>     All on a summer's day;

The Knave of Hearts he stole those tarts,
And took them clean away.

The King of Hearts called for those tarts,
And beat the Knave full sore.

The Knave of Hearts brought back those tarts,
And vowed he'd steal no more.

Mother Goose used only a few words, fifty-four to be exact, to tell us what we need to know about the Queen's tarts.

Many writers start writing a poem or a rhyming picture book and can't stop. Students have shown me poems that go on for thousands of words.

What a lot of work!

And for nothing!

Why nothing?

Remember we're writing for children with short attention spans. They can't sit still for long. *War and Peace* would never appeal to a five-year-old or even a ten-year-old. They simply can't focus on such a long, but fabulous, book.

So why do writers who rhyme go on too long?

## FOCUS

Sadly too many writers lose their focus. What is focus?

An advertising executive might say, "It's staying on message." It's not going off on tangents. It's following the poem, or story road, to the end without detours or side trips.

Notice *The Queen of Hearts* is only about the tarts being stolen and returned. It contains nothing about the argument the King and Queen had earlier that day. It neglects to mention the Knave, who already had a bad reputation for flirting with the milkmaids. And it doesn't include the Queen's recipe for tarts. These would all make fun separate poems, but they do not belong in this one.

There are two ways writers lose focus.

The first one is easy. *They don't have a focus to start with.* They're not sure what they're writing about and maybe even don't realize that they need to know. As we discussed in chapter 2, *Building a Frame for Your*

*Story House,* you, as the writer, must think about what you're trying to say. You don't need to state it in your writing, but you need to know what it is. Otherwise your writing will be like that house without any frame. It will collapse into the "so what?" variety. Or it will be a mere incident instead of a story.

In writing poetry, there's another way to lose one's focus. The writer starts having too much fun with the rhyme and forgets about the story, as I did here:

> The Queen of Hearts she made some tarts
>   As sweet as sweet can be
>
> and set them on a tray to serve
>   the King along with tea.
>
> "Oh, Yummy, yum," he said. "They're good.
>   I will eat them all."
>
> "No don't," she begged. "You'll grow so fat,
>   You won't fit through the hall.
>
> You need to share. Let's call the Knave.
>   You know he loves to eat."
>
> "He's not the kind of Knave I trust.
>   He'll steal each tasty treat."
>
> And so the King did as he planned
>   He gobbled up them all.
>
> Soon subjects searching for the King
>   found him trapped in the hall,
>
> conducting royal business there
>   because he was so wide.
>
> The Knave and Queen had lots of time
>   to wander and to hide
>
> beside the roses, near the tulips
>   They didn't ever miss

the King at all. They said sweet things
and stole a secret kiss.

That's how their torrid love began.
They couldn't help themselves.

Perhaps it was the flowers? Perhaps
some evil magic elves?

The Knave and Queen forced him away.
The King now lives alone.

His room is dark. His mood is bleak.
He only moans and groans.

The moral to this story is:
Heed well my words. Beware.

Loneliness shall come to you
if you don't ever share.

What happened here?

This began as a story about a Queen who made some tarts for the King. Then it moved into the King not sharing. Then the King grew fat. The Queen and Knave began to have a relationship, and I wrote a stanza to speculate about the cause. Last of all, I tacked on a moral.

I admit it was fun to write, but the focus changed with almost every stanza because each rhyme took me to a new place.

Rhyming is a great pleasure. There's nothing like opening up a rhyming dictionary and finding a word that takes you in new directions. But the writer has to stop and ask: What is the point? If the story is about stolen tarts, stick to those purloined pastries and nothing more.

# RHYME

As we've seen from the above example, rhyming, or the repetition of sounds, can be fun. Unfortunately many newcomers trying to write a rhyming picture book don't understand that rhyming must be **consistent**.

Let's look again at *The Queen of Hearts*.

| The Queen of Hearts she made some tarts, | (a) |
| All on a summer's day; | (b) |
| | |
| The Knave of Hearts he stole those tarts, | (a) |
| And took them clean away. | (b.1) |
| | |
| The King of Hearts called for those tarts, | (a) |
| And beat the Knave full sore. | (c) |
| | |
| The Knave of Hearts brought back those tarts, | (a) |
| And vowed he'd steal no more. | (c.1) |

Those letters at the end of the each line let you know which lines rhyme. You can see that we have a repetition of sound at the end of the lines. We have here an *abab, acac* pattern, or one in which every other line rhymes. If there is a number after the letter, as in the last line of the first stanza, that means the word rhymes with the *b* word that came before, but it is not the same word. If this stanza had another line that ended with the word *stay*, the appropriate designation would be *b.2*.

Unfortunately trying to maintain a consistent rhyme pattern leads beginning writers to make unwise word choices, such as using words that rhyme but don't add to the meaning of the poem or forced rhyme, as in the following example:

> The Queen of Hearts she made some tarts,
>  All on a summer's day;
>
> The Knave of Hearts he stole those tarts,
>  And took them all, <u>I say</u>.
>
> The King of Hearts called for those tarts,
>  And beat the Knave full sore.
>
> The Knave of Hearts brought back those tarts,
>  And vowed he'd steal no more.

If you're going to write a picture book in rhyme, you must make sure that *every word* moves your story forward. *I say* was obviously put there only to keep the rhyming pattern.

Rhyming leads to another problem. It can make your picture book poem too predictable. You don't want your reader to be able to guess every rhyming word. This usually happens when each line is a complete sentence, as in the following:

> The Queen of Hearts she made some tarts.
> She did on a summer's day.
>
> The Knave of Hearts he stole those tarts.
> He stole them clean away.
>
> The King of Hearts called for those tarts.
> He beat the Knave full sore.
>
> The Knave of Hearts brought back those tarts.
> He vowed he'd steal no more.

Create some spillover lines, which are sentences that don't always end when the line does, so your rhyming will not be so predictable. Reread the original poem to see examples of spillover lines.

Beginning writers striving for a perfect rhyme scheme often use unnatural sentence inversions, as in the following example:

> The Queen of Hearts she made some tarts,
> All on a summer's day;
>
> The Knave of Hearts he stole those tarts,
> <u>Tasty ones were they.</u>
>
> The King of Hearts called for those tarts,
> <u>And beat so hard the Knave</u>
>
> The Knave of Hearts brought back those tarts,
> <u>And the Knave the King forgave.</u>

In our rhymed picture books, we want the writing to sound as natural as normal conversation. While poets many years ago got away with sentence inversions, we are much stricter today. Don't let your poem sound stilted and old-fashioned.

If you are tempted to use either forced rhyme or unnatural sentence inversions to keep your rhyme consistent, resist the temptation!

But there's an opposite side to trying to keep to a regular rhyme pattern. Too often writers, not willing to spend the time or not aware

of how important it is to be consistent, break the rhyme pattern, as in the example below:

> The Queen of Hearts she made some tarts,
>   All on a summer's day;
>
> The Knave of Hearts he stole those tarts,
>   And took them clean away.
>
> The King of Hearts called for those tarts,
>   And beat the Knave full sore.
>
> The Knave of Hearts brought back those <u>sweets,</u>
>   <u>And vowed he'd learned his lesson.</u>

Why is this so jarring? Because the listener has accepted the pattern set up in the first stanza, not only in his ears, but also in his body. He expects this pattern to continue, in the same way we expect the sun to rise in the east and set in the west. Imagine what would happen if the sun suddenly rose in the north and set in the south! We would be thrown off balance big time. To a lesser degree, we were thrown off balance with the last rewrite of our Mother Goose poem.

You may rightfully wonder if there are times when it's okay to break the rhyme pattern.

Yes. But here's the catch.

You can't break the rhyme scheme just because you can't find a word that fits. *Only break the rhyme scheme to echo a change in the action of your poem.* For instance, if the action in your poem is slowing down, you might insert an extra line to echo that slower movement. If the action in your poem suddenly speeds up, you might delete a line, thereby bringing the rhymes closer together.

Often writers change the rhyme scheme at the end of a poem, or a rhymed picture book, to signal the finish, perhaps writing a nice rhyming couplet instead of an *abcb* pattern throughout the piece.

But it isn't only a lack of brevity, focus, and rhyme that makes editors groan over picture book manuscripts written as poems. Rhythm is a key element of successful rhymed picture books. But it's the element writers seem to have the most trouble understanding.

It's time to take a deep breath and remind yourself that you can do this. If I could learn this, believe me, you can, too.

# RHYTHM

As with rhyme, the key is ... *consistency.* Don't be fooled into thinking if you can count syllables, you have mastered rhythm.

Rhythm is *not* syllable count, it's counting *stresses* and *rhythmical feet.* Rhythm is a pattern of stresses and nonstresses. See how I have put slanted lines above the words to indicate the stresses and periods above the words for nonstresses.

     .   /  .  /  .  /  .  /
The Queen of Hearts she made some tarts,

     . / .  /    .
All on a summer's day;

    .  /  .  /  .  /  .  /
The Knave of Hearts he stole those tarts,

    .  /  .  /  .
And took them clean away.

    .  /  .  /  .  /  .  /
The King of Hearts called for those tarts,

    .  /  .  /  .  /
And beat the Knave full sore.

    .  /  .  /  .  /  .  /
The Knave of Hearts brought back those tarts,

    .  /  .  /  .  /
And vowed he'd steal no more.

In this poem, we have a soft beat followed by a stress, . /, otherwise known as an *iambic rhythm.* The soft beat and stress together form one *metrical foot.* In the lines above, the first, third, fifth, and seventh lines consist of four iambic metrical feet. The others (the second, fourth, sixth and eighth) have only three iambic feet to a line. While every

line does not have an equal number of feet, the overall poem has a repeated pattern of four feet, three feet, four feet, three feet, and so on. When you write a story in rhyme, you must create a consistent pattern in your number of feet, or else you will jar your reader as in the next example:

> The Queen of Hearts she made some tarts,
>     All on a summer's day;
>
> The Knave of Hearts he stole those tarts,
>     And took them clean away.
>
> The King of Hearts called for those tarts,
>     And beat the Knave full sore.
>
> The Knave of Hearts brought back those tarts,
>     <u>And vowed he'd never steal anything any more.</u>

Jarring can also happen by cutting out a beat, as in:

> The Queen of Hearts she made some tarts,
>     All on a summer's day;
>
> The Knave of Hearts he stole those tarts,
>     And took them clean away.
>
> The King of Hearts called for those tarts,
>     And beat the Knave full sore.
>
> The Knave of Hearts brought back those tarts,
>     <u>And stole no more.</u>

Let me emphasize that poetry written in a lockstep rhythm often needs to be broken, but only, and I stress this, *only* if it echoes a change in what's going on in the poem. Rhythm cannot be broken just because the poet needs to squeeze in some extra words.

Here's what happens when the writer uses no rhythmical pattern at all (different rhythms *and* different number of metrical feet) but sticks to a consistent rhyme scheme.

> The Queen of Hearts made a tray of tasty tarts.
>     She did it one hot summer day

138

The nasty Knave of Hearts stole every single one of those tarts,
He took them away.

The King of Hearts was disappointed and called for those tarts,
He beat the Knave until he was totally sore

The Knave of Hearts had no choice at all but to bring back the tarts.
He promised he'd never steal anything anymore.

I have to cover my ears reading this out loud. Can you hear how no rhythm translates to no poem?

Sometimes new writers use old-fashioned language to make the rhythm pattern consistent:

The Queen of Hearts she made some tarts,
'Twas on a summer's day;

The Knave of Hearts he stole those tarts,
And took them clean away.

The King of Hearts called for those tarts,
'Cause he so longed for sweets

The Knave of Hearts brought back those tarts,
And now has nil for eats.

Don't do this! It will make your poem out-of-date before your editor even reads it.

But let's assume you still want to write your picture book using rhythm and rhyme. Then you must become familiar and comfortable with the following four basic rhythms.

# Iambic

We saw an example of this in *The Queen of Hearts.*

Each iambic foot starts with a soft beat followed by a hard beat. A good way to remember it is by thinking of the nonsensical sounds *da DUM.* An iambic foot is designated by . /, the period and then the slash. It is considered an upbeat, rising, and happy rhythm; some examples are the words *today, against, remote,* or in the groups of words *the house, a pie, an elk.* It is the most commonly used rhythm, probably because it echoes our own heartbeat.

## Anapest

Each anapestic foot starts with two soft beats and ends with a hard beat. Its nonsensical sounds would be *da da DUM.* It would be designated with *. . /*, or two periods and then a slash. You will find it in the words *overwrite, interlock, disagree,* or the phrases *in the park, near the beach, a small cat.* This is an even happier, more upbeat rising rhythm than the iambic, and using it signals the reader you are writing something humorous. *The Night Before Christmas* by Clement Clarke Moore is almost a perfect anapestic poem.

Now let's move away from the upbeat rhythms to the falling rhythms.

## Trochee

Each trochaic foot starts with a hard beat followed by a soft beat. If you want to speak it in nonsensical sounds, you would say *DUM da.* It's designated first by a slash and then a period */ .*, and is found in the words *money, jiffy, digging,* and in the word groups *take her, read this, twirled a.* The trochee tends to be used in sadder, perhaps more serious, poems or writings.

## Dactyl

Each dactylic foot starts with one hard beat and is followed by two soft beats. If you wanted to speak it in nonsensical sounds, you would say *DUM da da.* Designate it with a slash and then two periods or */ . .*, and find it in words like *liftable, feathering, jocular,* and in the word groups *lemons and, after the, chasing him.* Obviously the heavy rhythm of this falling downbeat is most often found in poems that deal with serious matters. Check out the picture book *Everett Anderson's Goodbye,* a moving story/poem about a young boy coming to terms with his father's death, by Lucille Clifton. Notice that the main character's name is a double-dactyl, setting the tone for what is to come in the writing.

Now you have a quick overview of the four basic rhythms.

That wasn't so bad, was it? But be wary. If you want to write rhymed picture books, you must be able to differentiate between the rhythms and create them consistently. I would suggest that you clap each one out with your hands, pound on a drum, and then do what I did: Memorize poems in each of the rhythms. I recited them on my morning walks until I felt comfortable with each one. To help you do this, here are four of my poems about snails, each written in strict rhythmic meter.

## IAMBIC

### Snail's Poem

If only you could live like me,
I know you'd love it here down low,
I'm always going leisurely.
If only you could live like me—
twigs, pebbles, seeds—so much to see!
You miss it when you don't move slow.
If only you could live like me,
I know you'd love it here down low.

## ANAPEST

### Two Decorators

The small spider is swinging about in the dark
hanging doilies of lace from the bushes and trees,
while the snail down below has her own work to do.
See her swirling long streamers across every walk—
The snail's paints are star-silver. Spider's threads are moon-
    white.
Watch the two busy creatures. Together they're toiling
to decorate day with the colors of night.

## TROCHEE

### Twisted Trails

Snail, you're moving crooked,
weaving idly on the sidewalk.
Don't you have a destination?
Does it hold no riches or no wondrous treasure?
Tell me Snail, is moving slow your special pleasure?

141

## DACTYL

*Snail's Artistry*

Nibbling on ivy young Snail eats so tastefully
tiny small mouthfuls of sweet summer greenery—
munching and munching. He rarely eats wastefully.
Finishing everything. Snail's thankful attitude
leads him to scribble around the dull scenery,
pictures of silver, expressing his gratitude.

After you feel comfortable with these different rhythms, read lots of
poetry. Determine the predominant rhythm and mark their stresses.
It is imperative for rhythm to feel as comfortable as an old sock you
can slip on whenever necessary. If you're not sure where the stress
comes in a specific word, look it up in a dictionary.

However, the stress may fall differently depending on the word's
placement in the sentence. For example, the word *money* is a trochaic
word with the stress on the first syllable. But if the words preceding
and following it created the phrase *put money back*, the stress would be
on *put* and *back* with no stress on *money* at all. The best way to test the
rhythm of your lines is to read them out loud as if they were normal
sentences, not poetry. That way, you're more likely to hear where the
real stresses fall. Another approach is to ask someone else to read your
lines and pay close attention to where they put the stresses.

Ready for another quiz?

Here's one to see how well you know rhythm. Identify the rhythm
in these lines taken from different poems of mine.

1. Hairy, baby, lightly bounding ...

2. Pig dozes in a quilt of grime ...

3. German artillery ...

4. The old spotted giraffe has twelve necks and a half ...

5. Changing bobbins—filled for empty ...

6. I like to hide inside my den ...

7. Shoulders stooping, huge head drooping ...

8. Let it cloud! Let it rain!

9. Look at the wonderful scenery!

10. I wish … that I could be a bird and fly …

11. I hear news that this year you may bring Christmas cheer …

12. Lusciously edible …

And the answers are: 1. trochee 2. iambic 3. dactyl 4. anapest 5. trochee 6. iambic 7. trochee 8. anapest 9. dactyl 10. iambic 11. anapest 12. dactyl.

Perhaps you did well on this quiz and feel comfortable in rhyme. You've decided your picture book can stay in rhyme, but now you know the pitfalls.

Perhaps you've decided a poem picture book is not for you. You want to go back to prose.

## WHAT'S NEXT?

Writing your picture book in prose does not mean you can abandon poetry entirely. A picture book does not need to be a poem, but it must be written poetically, and we'll talk about how to do that in chapter 14.

## BEFORE YOU GO ON

1. If you've written your picture book in rhyme and want to keep it that way, go back over it line by line to be sure you haven't made any of the errors that drive editors to pull out their hair.

2. If you think poetry will be your thing but you want to read more, check out my favorite and most accessible books about writing poetry listed in the bibliography at the end of this book.

3. Maybe you've decided to forgo the poetry. Rewrite your story in prose and go on to the next chapter.

4. Read some picture books in rhyme. Here are few of my favorites:

- *Babies on the Go* by Linda Ashman
- *Bear Snores On* by Karma Wilson
- *Chicken Soup With Rice: A Book of Months* by Maurice Sendak
- *Everywhere Babies* by Susan Meyers
- *The Gruffalo* by Julia Donaldson
- *How Do You Make a Baby Smile?* by Philemon Sturges
- *The Lot at the End of My Block* by Kevin Lewis
- *Mama's Milk* by Michael Elsohn Ross
- *Sailing Off to Sleep* by Linda Ashman
- *Tattered Sails* by Verla Kay
- *There Was a Wee Woman ...* by Erica Silverman
- *Who Likes Rain?* by Wong Herbert Yee
- *Wild About Books* by Judy Sierra
- *Yertle the Turtle and Other Stories* by Dr. Seuss

# MAKING MUSIC
# WITH YOUR PROSE

*Every word only has to
be perfect.* —*Ursula Nordstrom*

If you've decided to stay away from poetry and write your picture book in prose, that does not mean you can skip this chapter and avoid all contact with poetry. If you do, you run the chance of having your manuscript rejected by an editor. Theodore Geisel, more famously known as Dr. Seuss, said: "Write a verse a day, not to send to publishers, but to throw in wastebaskets. It will help your prose. It will give you swing. Shorten paragraphs and sentences, then shorten words…. Use verbs. Let the kids fill in the adjectives …"

Poems are our shortest and tightest form of writing. Every word counts.

Every word must also count in our picture books. Each word needs to be the best word for moving the story forward and for echoing the action in the story. Remember Mark Twain's statement: "The difference between the right word and the almost-right word is the difference between lightning and a lightning-bug." Here are two attributes to help you determine the right word.

## RHYTHM

In our last chapter, we talked about the rhythm of words. Some words ended with a stress, while others ended with a soft beat. The words that

ended with a stress were called upbeat rhythms, or *iambic* and *anapest*. The words that ended with a soft beat were called falling rhythms, or *trochee* and *dactyl*.

When you write in prose, you still need to be aware of these rhythms, but you don't need to write your entire story in one of them. Certain sections will call for different rhythms. Let's look at some examples.

In her picture storybook *The Christmas Miracle of Jonathan Toomey*, Susan Wojciechowski gave her main character a dactylic first name and a trochaic second name. Then in the middle of the first paragraph she states:

> He [Jonathan Toomey] went about mumbling and grumbling, muttering and sputtering, grumping and griping. He complained that the church bells rang too often, that the birds sang too shrilly, that the children played too loudly.

Take note of the falling rhythms of many words in these two sentences. Also notice how Wojciechowski ends each sentence with a soft beat.

Can't you feel the heaviness and the sadness of these words? Even if she had written her book in a foreign language and you couldn't understand a word, you'd still know the falling rhythms suggest a book that will not be full of jokes and laughter. It's a serious book about a serious topic.

Let's look at Natasha Wing's *Go to Bed, Monster!*

> One night, Lucy tossed and turned. She could not, would not, did not want to go to bed.

Compare the music of these two sentences to those from Wojciechowski's book. Each of Wing's sentences ends with a stress. The second sentence is a perfect *iambic* line with the stresses on *could, would, did, want, go,* and *bed*. Writing the words in that way gave the appropriate stress to Lucy's strong feelings. You can almost hear her stamping her feet for emphasis. The upbeat rhythm lets the listener know she is not going to hear a sad book. This book feels fun, just by the choice of the rhythm.

Sentence length is also an important part of rhythm. Compare the two excerpts above and see how *Go to Bed, Monster!* makes use of short, punchy sentences. *The Christmas Miracle of Jonathan Toomey* uses longer and more leisurely sentences to encourage the reader to slow down and contemplate the story.

While thinking about the rhythm of words and sentences, you'll also want to think about another aspect of words.

# THE SOUNDS OF LETTERS

Become familiar with the sounds of every letter of the alphabet. Do this experiment: Hold your hand close to your mouth, but not touching your lips. Say the sounds of each letter, and pay attention to the difference in breath on your hand and to the shape of your mouth. For example, when I say the *a* sound in *sat*, I feel little breath on my hand. My mouth stays open. However, when I say *a* as in *day*, my lower lip raises, which explains the bigger puff of air on my hand.

When you do this through the entire alphabet, you will get a sense of those letter sounds that create the biggest puffs on your hand. The bigger the puffs, the harder and stronger the sounds. The shorter puffs are softer and weaker.

Here's a chart to help you remember:

### *Low Range—Less Energy Vowel Sounds*

| | |
|---|---|
| oo | soon |
| o | bone |
| aw | bought |
| oi | toy |
| ow | chow |
| ah | far |

### *Middle Range Vowel Sounds*

| | |
|---|---|
| u | club |
| e | herd |
| a | cat |
| e | hen |
| i | swim |

### High Range Vowel Sounds

| | |
|---|---|
| i | bright |
| a | play |
| ee | tree |

### Hard Sound Consonants

B, D, K, P, Q, T, and hard C

### Softer, Liquid Consonant Sounds

L, M, N, and R

How do these sounds apply to your story?

Here are some writers who made excellent use of letter sounds as related to the tone of their picture books:

From *Owl Moon* by Jane Yolen:

> Somewhere behind us
> a train whistle blew,
> long and low,
> like a sad, sad song.

We've talked about how the use of long sentences clues the reader she's entering into a more leisurely read. Also notice here the larger number of low and middle range vowels compared to the lesser number of high range vowels. See how the author uses *L*s and *S*s and *N*s. My favorite part of this sentence is: *long and low, like a sad, sad song.* Surely a story about being quiet late at night searching for owls calls for a dreamy mood.

A different mood is created by hard sounds. Erica Silverman, in her story picture book *Sholom's Treasure: How Sholom Aleichem Became a Writer*, gives us some of Sholom's stepmother's curses. One of them goes like this:

> May you ache and break! Peak and pine and split your spine!

All those hard sounds of *K* and *B* and *P* and *T* and the long *A*, *E*, and *I* sounds confirm that these are curses. When wishing someone well, the sounds would be softer, more gentle and loving.

Read picture books, paying close attention to how the authors used word sounds and rhythm to echo the action and mood of the story.

Now take a break and make sure you understand the different uses of word sounds and rhythm and how to use them in your story.

## Rhythm and Word Sound Quiz

1. When writing about a boy chasing a horse, what kind of sentences, long or short, might you use?

2. You are writing a quiet bedtime story. What specific rhythm should you avoid?

3. Your character sits down by a stream to daydream. What kind of sentences, long or short, would you write?

4. A very silly story would use what kind of rhythms?

5. In a wild action scene, what word sounds, high and hard or low and soft, would you want to use?

6. Your main character is at a circus, turning from one ring to the other, looking at the clowns, the elephants, the lions,. What kind of sentences, long or short, would reflect her actions?

7. Your story is about a boy adjusting to the death of his dog. What kind of sentences, long or short; rhythms, upbeat or falling; and word sounds, low and soft or high and hard, would you write?

8. What kind of sentences, long or short, would best express the action of a story in which a kitten is lost and a frantic search is on?

9. Long-awaited good news has finally arrived. What kind of sentences, long or short, would demonstrate the excitement?

10. In a high action story when the chase is on, which of these two words might you use: *dart* or *run*? Why?

11. Your story takes place near a quiet pond. What word sounds, low and soft or high and hard, might you use? Give a few examples of some words that might fit.

12. The stream is moving quickly. What consonant and vowel sounds, low and soft or high and hard, might you use?

Answers: 1. short sentences 2. the lively and upbeat anapest 3. long sentences 4. iambic and anapest—the upbeat rhythms 5. hard sounds and high vowels 6. short sentences 7. long sentences, falling rhythms and low, soft sounds to echo the sadness 8. short sentences 9. short sentences 10. dart because of its hard sounds 11. low vowels and liquid sounds like flow, linger, ramble 12. harder consonants and higher vowels, along with shorter sentences.

Just because you're not a poet doesn't mean you can't use some poetic tools. They're free for the using to all writers.

# ALLITERATION

This is the repetition of the initial consonant sounds of words in a succession, such as *long, low lullaby.*

Using too many too close together can turn a sentence into a tongue twister and a nightmare for your reader. Think of *Peter Piper picked a peck of pickled peppers.* Remember, our picture books are meant to be read out loud, so our words need to flow off the reader's tongue. Notice there's still alliteration in this: *A young boy, Peter Piper, went to the garden to pick some peppers for his mother to pickle.* Isn't it much easier to read? Weaving alliteration throughout the longer sentence is gentler to the tongue and the ear. Depending on what you are writing, you might want to keep your alliteration tight. Other times you might drop it in at intervals to be more subtle.

You'll find an example of alliteration in *So You Want to Be President* by Judith St. George when she lists foods served at a dinner party:

...turtle soup, oysters, beef, turkey, mutton chops, chicken...

The alliterative words come far apart with *turtle* and *turkey*, and right next to each other with *chops, chicken.*

# ASSONANCE

This is the repetition of vowel sounds in succession, as in: Sweep streets clean.

You can pick up the long *e* sounds here, can't you? But you also can make the sounds more subtle but still with impact. *Would you sweep the street in front of our house clean?*

Alice Schertle, the author of *Very Hairy Bear*, uses assonance twice when she writes: "KERPLUNK! He'll even dunk his no hair nose." The short *U* sound is repeated, as is the long *O* sound.

# CONSONANCE

This poetic tool repeats the same middle and end sounds as in *fat cat sat* or beginning and ending consonants in a word sequence such as *click, clack* or *sniffle, snuffle*. Again it's acceptable to spread those words out in a sentence in prose. He heard the click and then the clack of the train coming down the track.

# ONOMATOPOEIA

Words imitate sounds in this poetic tool. *Buzz, tick-tock, swish, quack,* and *woof* are all examples. Kids and adults love onomatopoetic words. They're easy and fun because the reader can naturally add stress and dramatic flare.

Jim Aylesworth employed lots of onomatopoetic words in *Country Crossing.*

> PUTTAPUTT PUTT PUTT PUTT.
> PUTTAPUTT PUTT PUTT PUTT,
> went the old motor. And
> CHURRRRRR
> went the tires on the pavement.

That's it! Time for another quiz. What poetic tools are used in these phrases? Alliteration, assonance, consonance, or onomatopoeia.

1. Hip! Hop!
2. Stay still

3. Beep! Beep!

4. Green grass

5. Run in the sun

6. Smash! Crash!

7. Down on the ground

8. Smack smock

And the answers are: 1. consonance 2. alliteration 3. onomatopoeia 4. alliteration 5. assonance 6. onomatopoeia 7. assonance 8. consonance.

Now we have three more poetic tools that have nothing to do with word sounds and repetition.

## METAPHOR

When a writer uses metaphor, she says one thing is actually something else, as in: *Writing is a journey through a long, dark tunnel.* Douglas Wood uses metaphors in his book *Old Turtle.* The elements and creatures are arguing about God. The star says, "God is a twinkling and a shining, far, far away. But the antelope says, "God is a runner, swift and free, who loves to leap and race with the wind."

Floyd Cooper speaks in metaphor in *Coming Home: From the Life of Langston Hughes* when he calls a train the old iron snake.

## SIMILE

Here the writer compares one thing to another with the words like or as. An example would be: I was as mad as the bumblebee Ferdinand sat on.

Eileen Spinelli uses simile in her humorous book *Something to Tell the Grandcows.* Emmadine, the cow, was experiencing the South Pole for the first time and "Her teeth chattered like spoons." Here's another simile from *Rupa Raises the Sun* by Marsha Wilson Chall: "the sun broke across the sky like an egg yolk."

We write in metaphor and simile to give the reader a visual image instead of a plain description. An added benefit is that metaphors and similes cut down on the words necessary to describe what we're trying to get across. Consider *Writing is a journey through a long, dark tunnel.*

How might I describe this without the metaphor? I'd have to write about how, when I start a story, I don't always know where I'm going. I experiment with all different possibilities but often can't see what will work. Sometimes I try one direction, then another and on, and on, and on. You can imagine what a long and detailed account is required to get across what my metaphor does is one short sentence.

Whether you're creating a metaphor or a simile, make sure you are not writing a cliché. *Still as a statue* and *black as night* have been done to death. While you might write a cliché in your first draft, when you revise consider whether it is the best you can do. Remember what Mark Twain said about the right word. The same applies to the right metaphor or simile.

You want to write your similes and metaphors in language appropriate to the time and setting of the story. For example, in a story taking place on the prairie, you wouldn't want to say the fox raced away fast as an airplane. A far more appropriate way of putting it might be: the fox raced fast as a tornado.

How do you create unique, visual, and tone-perfect metaphors and similes? There's no magic way.

This method works best for me: I number 1 to 10 on a piece of paper or on my computer and free associate until I have ten possibilities. If I like one of them, I'm done. If I don't like any of them, I number from 11 to 20. I go on and on until I finally create one that seems exactly right.

Do I hear a moan? Hush!

Writing is time-consuming, but the time spent is worthwhile. Remember we're not just cranking our stories out. We're creating compelling early-book experiences for our listeners.

# PERSONIFICATION

With this tool we give human characteristics to something that is not human. *The book held me in its grasp until the final page.* A book has no arms to hold me, but I still can't put it down.

Some other examples of personification would be:

The breeze whispered secrets with the leaves.
Fear tapped me on the shoulder.
Lonliness, my only friend, walked me to school.

Ready for another quiz? Let's see how well you understand metaphor, simile, and personification.

1. The moon is a bowl of breakfast cereal.

2. I ran, but danger ran faster.

3. Jake did not want to go to Bill's party, so he moved slow as a snail.

4. Molly felt like a bear caught in a trap.

5. The tree is our umbrella, keeping us dry from the rain.

6. The quilt spoke stories of love and loss.

Answers: 1. metaphor 2. personification 3. simile 4. simile 5. metaphor, 6. personification.

If you didn't do as well as you'd like on the quizzes in this chapter, you might study some of the following poets. Reading and studying poetry was the best thing I did for myself as a picture book writer. The list doesn't contain children's poets exclusively. The more poets you read, no matter what genre or age they write for, the more poetic your writing will become. Here are some of my favorites, including one of my own:

- *All by Herself* by Ann Whitford Paul
- *All the Small Poems* by Valerie Worth
- *America, My New Home* by Monica Gunning
- *Ancient Voices* by Kate Hovey
- *Animal Stackers* by Jennifer Belle
- *Balloons and Other Poems* by Deborah Chandra
- *Been to Yesterdays: Poems of a Life* by Lee Bennett Hopkins
- *Black Swan/White Crow* by J. Patrick Lewis
- *A Book of Americans* by Rosemary and Stephen Vincent Benet
- *Candy Corn* by James Stevenson
- *Celebrations* by Myra Cohn Livingston
- *A Child's Garden of Verses* by Robert Louis Stevenson

- *The Dream Keeper and Other Poems* by Langston Hughes
- *Everett Anderson's Goodbye* by Lucille Clifton
- *Everything Glistens and Everything Sings: New and Selected Poems* by Charlotte Zolotow
- *Fireflies at Midnight* by Marilyn Singer
- *Girl Coming in for a Landing: A Novel in Poems* by April Halprin Wayland
- *Good Luck Gold and Other Poems* by Janet S. Wong
- *How Now, Brown Cow?* by Alice Schertle
- *If I Were in Charge of the World and Other Worries* by Judith Viorst
- *I'm Small and Other Verses* by Lilian Moore
- *It's About Dogs* by Tony Johnston
- *Joyful Noise: Poems for Two Voices* by Paul Fleischman
- *Keeping the Night Watch* by Hope Anita Smith
- *Lemonade Sun and Other Summer Poems* by Rebecca Kai Dotlich
- *A Light in the Attic* by Shel Silverstein
- *Mites to Mastodons: A Book of Animal Poems* by Maxine Kumin
- *My House Is Singing* by Betsy R. Rosenthal
- *Old Elm Speaks: Tree Poems* by Kristine O'Connell George
- *On the Wing* by Douglas Florian
- *One at a Time* by David McCord
- *The Pedaling Man and Other Poems* by Russell Hoban
- *The Poetry of Robert Frost* by Robert Frost
- *A Sky Full of Poems* by Eve Merriam
- *The Song in My Head* by Felice Holman
- *Spin a Soft Black Song* by Nikki Giovanni
- *Splish Splash* by Joan Bransfield Graham
- *Stop Pretending: What Happened When My Big Sister Went Crazy* by Sonya Sones
- *Tyrannosaurus Was a Beast* by Jack Prelutsky
- *Under the Tree* by Elizabeth Madox Roberts
- *Voyages* by Walt Whitman

Also check out the books mentioned in this chapter. Many of them use several different poetic tools in their stories. When you feel comfortable recognizing the way the poet uses rhythm and word sounds, and the different poetic tools, you'll begin to think about how you, too, can use them in your stories.

## WHAT'S NEXT?

We've been talking about language in the last two chapters—now we'll turn to the last point to consider, which is word count. Get ready to do some serious cutting on your picture book manuscript.

## BEFORE YOU GO ON

1. Go over your manuscript. Did you use any of these poetic techniques? If not, can you improve your manuscript by doing so?

2. Check your published books to see how the authors use the tools discussed here.

3. Read a new picture book.

# CHAPTER 15

# THE IMPORTANCE OF WORD COUNT

*In composing, as a general rule, run your pen through every other word you have written; you have no idea what vigor it will give to your style.* —*Sydney Smith*

Beginning picture book writers often have no comprehension of how few words are necessary to reach their young audience. Who would believe, for example, that the classic *Goodnight Moon* by Margaret Wise Brown needed only 130 words to tell the comforting story of a bunny bidding good night to his room and its contents? Think of it! Only 130 words.

Rarely do I see a student manuscript that some serious cutting couldn't improve. Don't be like the speaker who, finally given the podium, has so much fun in front of the audience he doesn't know when to stop. Don't allow the tumor of too-many-words to invade your brain and spread disease to your story.

In order to be a tumor-free writer of picture books, you must have the following attributes.

## A FULL UNDERSTANDING OF THE ILLUSTRATOR'S JOB

The illustrator's pictures are the narrative of our words. That's why we don't need to write long descriptions. The pictures will show

what the character looks like. They will show the setting. Trust the creativity of the artist.

Linda Zuckerman, a former editor and now a children's book author, often asks the writers in conference audiences to imagine what a mousery—a place where mice live—might look like. Some people suggest a Victorian dollhouse. Others say an old trunk, or perhaps a hatbox. Then Linda holds up *The Mousery* by Charlotte Pomerantz and Kurt Cyrus for all to see. The mousery Cyrus envisioned was, in fact, an old abandoned car. Throughout my career, I've been overwhelmed with the creativity of illustrators.

Writers don't have to write directions for what each picture should be. In fact, they need to leave room for the illustrator to add her story in pictures.

Ironically, while we must write with a visual image in our mind, we must eventually let that image go. When we send our children to school, we allow teachers, friends, the crosswalk guard, the grocery store clerk, and the whole wide world to help shape our daughters and sons into adults. We trust all will be well. We need to have that same trust in our illustrators. They will help each story grow into its fullest self.

None of my books came out the way I imagined they would. Every one of them came out *better*! So delete descriptions and your illustrator will love you. Chances are they will be ignored anyway. Whenever the talented artist Marla Frazee gets a manuscript from an editor to consider illustrating, the first thing she does is take a thick black marker and cross out any of the writer's picture suggestions.

# RESPECT FOR CHILDREN'S INTELLIGENCE

For our young listeners to fully comprehend a text, you must not make the mistake of explaining everything in excruciating detail. There's no need to tack on a moral, or lesson, for listeners to take away from your book. I can't repeat this enough. Please, writers, give children credit for their cognitive abilities. While kids' world experiences can't begin to compare to adults' in number, they have the same eyes and ears and brains for figuring things out. A child will take longer to verbalize the theme of a book, but that doesn't mean he doesn't understand the theme on some level deep inside.

Get rid of words that carry any hint of a moral, such as:

Jimmy learned never to lie again.
Becky decided the best way to be friends was to share.
Lora knew she would always love her baby brother.

## UNDERSTANDING AND SYMPATHY FOR YOUR READER AND LISTENER

Remember, children with short attention spans are listening to our stories. Have compassion for the adult reader reading out loud to others.

Children respond best to books that take into account their developmental stages. These days, doctors and reading specialists are encouraging parents and child-care workers to read to children as soon as they are born. But not *Crime and Punishment!*

Start babies out with board books. Their bright and simple illustrations are easy for young eyes to focus on. These books require few, if any, words, and their brevity accommodates a child's wiggles and squirms and his inability to concentrate for an extended period of time. Children under eighteen months discover their world through their senses, so it is natural to stuff books in their mouths. Normal, thin paper pages are simply objects to tear and crumple. Board books take this into account and are made of sturdy materials.

Babies and toddlers love the feel and texture of books, which makes *Pat the Bunny* by Dorothy Kunhardt and other touch-and-feel books so popular. Board books for children this age usually contain eight double-sided cardboards or sixteen pages, including the front and back covers. Additional pages can be added, if needed.

What does a board book for children under two look like?

The illustrations are one-dimensional and in bright, flat colors. They have few details and the text is short, with no more than a line or two on each page. Sometimes these books are wordless. Sometimes they have just one word.

A board book about fish might be as simple as a few words on a page like:

Little Fish swims.
Little Fish blows big bubbles.
Little Fish blows little bubbles.
Little Fish eats.
Look out, Little Fish!
Shark!
Swim fast, Little Fish!
That was close, Little Fish.

Here are the titles and word counts of a few of my favorite published board books:

- *Easter Egg Hunt* by Chuck Murphy, 36 words
- *Counting With Wayne Thiebaud* by Susan Goldman Rubin, 62 words
- *I Love You, Sun. I Love You, Moon* by Karen Pandell, 64 words
- *Zoom City* by Thacher Hurd, 66 words
- *Binky* by Leslie Patricelli, 80 words
- *Big Dog and Little Dog* by Dav Pilkey, 82 words

Publishers today have begun reprinting popular picture books in board book format, but don't be fooled. While some successfully make that transition, the majority do not. It is rare for a child under eighteen months to sit still for an entire read of most of these. A child nearing two might show the required patience, but usually these transformed books are merely a marketing ploy to extend the audience of a book without an awareness of the skills of small children.

Books for older toddlers and preschoolers can be longer because they have learned how to sit still for increasing amounts of time. Many of these books show a separate story in the pictures. In my book *Hello Toes! Hello Feet!*, I never mentioned a dog in the text. The illustrator, Nadine Bernard Westcott, added the small, cuddly dog so listeners could follow his actions and "read the pictures."

These books need to have a simple story line. When I say simple, I do not mean simplistic. I mean the story must be focused without too many issues or too many characters. Repetition and rhyme allows the listener to anticipate what's coming, and after several readings she might even say some of the words in advance. This age group of children likes stories pertaining to the world around them. And they like to hear a familiar story more than once, rather than listen to a new long story. That's why these stories are short, as you can see by the word count of some picture books listed below:

- *Whose Mouse Are You?* by Robert Kraus, 107 words
- *Bears in Pairs* by Niki Yektai, 122 words
- *Hello Toes! Hello Feet!* by Ann Whitford Paul, 217 words
- *A Mouse Told His Mother* by Bethany Roberts, 244 words
- *The Napping House* by Audrey Wood, 268 words
- *Little Monkey Says Good Night* by Ann Whitford Paul, 271 words
- *Up in the Air* by Myra Cohn Livingston, 308 words
- *Owl Babies* by Martin Waddell, 325 words
- *Nice Try, Tooth Fairy* by Mary W. Olson, 341 words
- *Night Noises* by Mem Fox, 361 words
- *The Treasure* by Uri Shulevitz, 371 words
- *My Mama Had a Dancing Heart* by Libba Moore Gray, 373 words
- *Miss Malarkey Doesn't Live in Room 10* by Judy Finchler, 380 words
- *Click, Clack, Moo: Cows That Type* by Doreen Cronin, 408 words
- *Everything to Spend the Night* by Ann Whitford Paul, 457 words
- *Tacky the Penguin* by Helen Lester, 461 words
- *Homeplace* by Anne Shelby, 466 words
- *Owen* by Kevin Henkes, 466 words
- *The Tale I Told Sasha* by Nancy Willard, 472 words
- *Froggy Gets Dressed* by Jonathan London, 475 words
- *That's Good! That's Bad* by Margery Cuyler, 478 words
- *Country Crossing* by Jim Aylesworth, 659 words
- *Two Mrs. Gibsons* by Toyomi Igus, 685 words
- *The Big Green Pocketbook* by Candice Ransom, 690 words
- *Big Pumpkin* by Erica Silverman, 693 words
- *Teddy Bear Tears* by Jim Aylesworth, 843 words

When I am writing for this age group, my antennae perk up at 700 words. I look for ways to cut or, if the topic is more advanced, I realize I'm writing for an older audience and revise accordingly by expanding my story into a picture storybook for an elementary age student.

A book about fish for the toddler-preschool age group could be a rhymed concept book about some aspect of fish who live in the ocean. A simple story might take one fish who longs to sun on the sand. It would show how he tries to achieve that goal and what happens to him afterward.

Once children are in kindergarten and elementary school, and practicing their sitting and listening skills, their stories can be longer and more complicated. Here are some sample books with word counts that are appropriate for the elementary school-age child:

- *Cleversticks* by Bernard Ashley, 660 words
- *Mañana, Iguana* by Ann Whitford Paul, 675 words
- *The Spider Who Created the World* by Amy MacDonald, 681 words
- *Tyrannosaurus Tex* by Betty G. Birney, 848 words
- *How I Became a Pirate* by Melinda Long, 951 words
- *The Wednesday Surprise* by Eve Bunting, 981 words
- *Heat Wave* by Helen Ketteman, 1022 words
- *A Regular Flood of Mishap* by Tom Birdseye, 1113 words
- *Bubba the Cowboy Prince: A Fractured Texas Tale* by Helen Ketteman, 1151 words
- *Saving Sweetness* by Diane Stanley, 1413 words
- *A Day's Work* by Eve Bunting, 1573 words
- *Sweet Clara and the Freedom Quilt* by Deborah Hopkinson, 2142 words

Notice that some of these books by word count alone could be a straight picture book for preschoolers. I've put them in this category because the subject matter was more suitable for elementary school children.

Going back to our story about a fish ... consider the classic folktale of the fisherman and his wife who lived in a sty near the sea. One day the fisherman caught a magic fish who offered to grant him a wish if he will throw him back to the sea. The kindhearted fisherman, without asking for a wish, unhooked him from the line and tossed him into the water. His wife, on hearing this, sent her husband back to wish for a hut. She was happy in her hut for a while, but then sent her husband back again to ask the fish for a great stone castle, and after that she asked for the power of a king and then of an emperor. At that request, the fish grew angry and sent them both back to their sty. This tale of greed and dissatisfaction clearly needs child listeners who have had more life experiences than toddlers.

But don't take my word about subject matter and word count in picture books. Do your own research. Read to children and find out for yourself how long their attention spans last. The painful experience of watching girls and boys squirm while listening to your published story can be avoided if you know what works and what doesn't for your intended audience. Volunteer at your local library, public school, or neighborhood day care center. Observe how long children of different ages sit still and listen. See when they start fidgeting or talking to the person next to them.

Then type up those stories that held the kids' interest.

Don't groan.

Typing manuscripts is the best practice for knowing in your head and in your fingers how long stories should be. My computer is filled with texts of published picture books. If you're like me, you'll be surprised by how few words are needed to tell a story.

I'll bet your manuscript (especially if you are just starting to write) is longer than it should be. In fact, many of my students' manuscripts benefit from being cut in half. When I assign my students to do such serious cutting, they ask, "How?"

To shrink your tumor of too-many-words, we've already discussed deleting descriptions and morals. Here are more specific suggestions.

**1. Cut adjectives and adverbs.** We don't need lots of adjectives. Cross off words like *beautiful*, *ugly*, and *smart* in your manuscript. Let your illustrator create a beautiful or ugly character.

Writing also comes to life when you delete adverbs and instead use more specific verbs. Not long ago, in rereading a manuscript of mine, I discovered I kept repeating the verb *run*. Sometimes I qualified it with *runs ahead fast*, *runs quickly*, *takes his time running*, but over and over again that dull word *run*. I cut out all those adverbs and replaced the verb with one that was more specific. *Runs ahead fast* became *dashes*. *Runs quickly* became *bolts*. And *takes his time running* became *jogs*.

A thesaurus works wonders in reminding writers of the incredible depth and breadth of our English language. The "right" word exists for every moment in our stories, and we owe it to our audience not to settle for less.

**2. Use active instead of passive verbs.** Lena sang a song is much more active than The song was sung by Lena. In the first sentence, the noun Lena is doing the singing. In the second sentence, the song is being sung by her, so the noun is not performing the action. Not only is the first sentence more active, it also needs fewer words.

Here's another passive sentence. *The game was won by the home team.* To make it more immediate, active, and stronger, and also using fewer words, this could be revised to read: *The home team won the game.* Every time we change a passive verb to an active verb, we are cutting out words. Hooray!

There are, of course, times when the passive form of the verb is needed, but be sure it is truly necessary.

**3. Cut out repetitive words.** Some repetitive words are critical for the rhythm and music of a story. Leave those in. Reading out loud is the best way to pick up repetitive phrases that don't enhance your story but, in fact, slow it down. Those words must be deleted. Even though we're not writing a poem, we're writing the closest thing to it. Each word must count and move the story ahead. So read your story to your dog, your cat, or your empty room until you have discovered and removed those extraneous words.

**4. Remove qualifying words**. Look out for *really, nearly, almost,* and *seems.* Stand behind what you write. You've done your research. You know what's true. Don't hide under these hem-and-haw words. What you say is either true, or not. There's no middle road.

**5. Get rid of wasted words.** You say, "I don't write wasted words." Phooey! We all write wasted words. Remember those term papers? How many times did you go over the word limit? If you were like me, rarely, if ever. So what did you do? You padded your report. You made longer sentences, you explained each concept several times.

But now you're writing picture books and faced with the opposite situation—too many words! Wasted words are any that don't move your story forward. If your main character is a bunny in search of his mother, do we need to know his thoughts about his best friend, too? No matter how beautifully that section is written, it needs to go in the wastebasket.

Ann Hoppe said: The words must be chipped away and chipped away so that only the essential few needed to carry the narrative forward and give it its unique flavor remain. The writer's job is to pare a story or experience down until the essence remains, spare and shining.

**6. Jettison the justs.** *A lucky penny sat just one foot away.* Get rid of *just*—A lucky penny sat one foot away. Granted times will come in your writing when you want to emphasize with just, but I've found it tends to be a word thrown in without thinking. Most *justs* can be eliminated.

**7. There were, it is, it was, it isn't.** These, or any words like them, at the beginning of sentences can easily be cut. Why not rewrite: There were three bears sitting on chairs to Three bears were sitting on chairs, or even better, Three bears sat on chairs.

These words are a signal to me to stop and try to combine the sentence with the one that came before. For instance *Jerry found his wallet. It was on the table in the hall.* would be better as *Jerry found his wallet on the table in the hall.*

**8. See, hear, watch, look.** Check your manuscript to see if these words are necessary. When a story is told from Jimmy's point of view, do we need to say He saw Mother standing at the door? It's redundant because we already know Jimmy is telling us the story. He obviously is the one who is seeing her. Again, for emphasis, you might want to leave it in, but in my experience many of these words can be discarded.

**9. Do you need both an attribution and an action?** *"Let go of me," Jessica said. She squirmed. "I'm going to tell Dad."*

This could be written with only the attribution of who's speaking. *"Let go of me," Jessica said. "I'm going to tell Dad."* Or alternatively, use the action only: *"Let go of me." Jessica squirmed. "I'm going to tell Dad."*

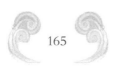

165

**10. Which is a witch.** Certain words raise my dander. *Which* is one of them. Why write *She ran to school, which is two blocks away?* A smoother sentence would be *She ran two blocks to school.*

**11. Don't be an owl—get rid of who-oo's.** *Who* is another word that sprouts my dander even higher. *Steve, who was racing to the finish line, sensed victory.* A tighter and more exciting way to write it would be *Racing to the finish line, Steve sensed victory.*

**12. Don't double dip.** Assuming that a verb is strong, we don't need to add emphasis to it with an adverb that says the same thing.

In the sentence *Bill stomped away angrily*, we know that stomping away shouts out ANGRY. Delete the adverb.

**13. Two is not better than one.** It's easier to write a string of adjectives or actions when one will suffice. Sentences like the following come from the writer thinking more is better, but also having trouble deciding which word, or words, to use. See how each one is improved by choosing the best.

The lion showed his horrible, sharp, glistening white teeth.

Here's the shorter version: *The lion showed his sharp teeth.*
In this sentence the writer used several verbs.

She jumped up and down and shouted for joy.

Both verbs express joy.

She jumped up and down. She shouted for joy.

Pick your favorite.

**14. Characters don't pee in stories.** What this means is we don't need every detail of their lives.

When you're cutting, look for spots where you've written more activities than necessary. The sentences *Laura stood up, walked across the room to the door. She turned the knob. She opened the door and then went outside* could be cut to just three words, *Laura went outside.*

At dramatic moments in your story, you might want to slow the action down and put in all of these steps, but usually they can be combined into one action.

**15. Cut out purple prose.** Don't write *Seeing him, her heart thumped louder than a drum, louder than a train engine, louder than a rock concert, loud enough so the moon and stars could hear it.*

We mistakenly think the more we say and the greater we exaggerate, the more likely we are to make our point. Instead our point gets hidden behind so many words. The reader may say to herself, *That's ridiculous!* and close the book. Try to come up with something more possible, and original, or pick just one description.

**16. Don't show *and* tell.** This often comes from a writer's insecurity. He wonders whether the reader and listener will get what he's saying, so he says it twice.

> When she saw her broken piggy bank, she started to cry. She was sad.

Obviously in this circumstance the girl would not be crying with joy. Delete the telling statement *She was sad.*

Mary Calhoun said, "Writing a picture book story involves all the focusing and intensity and control of writing a poem." The way to get that focus is to get rid of each word that doesn't move your story forward. Tighten your story. Gear it to your audience and cross out any word that doesn't carry its weight.

Want some practice before you tackle your own? See how many writing mistakes you can pick up in my Sammy Skunk story (mentioned at the beginning of the book). I've expanded it and made it even worse for the purpose of this exercise.

### Sammy Skunk Saves the Day

Charlie Chipmunk's birthday was fast approaching. It was Monday and he was so excited. Charlie Chipmunk got out four pieces paper and crayons and drew a picture of a red and blue balloon and then he wrote *Please come to my Birthday Party,* and added the date and the time and folded it neatly and then last of all he put each invitation into an envelope and sealed it shut. Then he went to deliver the invitations for his birthday party. On the way, he thought about his Mother and wished she could come to celebrate with him.

He put one under Oliver Opossum's log. He put another just near Robert Rabbit's hole. And he shouted across the pond to Billy Beaver. "Come get your invitations to my party."

Last of all Charlie put an invitation into the opening of Sammy Skunk's rock pile.

But as he went back to his burrow, Charlie remembered Sammy Skunk's horrible smell.

"Sammy can't come to my party," he cried. "Whenever he gets scared he lets out that horrible smell. What if he gets scared at my party?"

Charlie Chipmunk remembered the time last spring when he and Sammy Skunk were playing under a tree and a bird dropped a twig that landed right on Sammy Skunk's cute little black nose. Skunk jumped and "Whew!" They had to go play in the meadow.

"Oh no! How could I have forgotten Sammy's smell." Chipmunk cried. He stomped his paw. "Skunk will ruin my party."

Chipmunk raced back to Sammy's rock pile, which took him ten minutes. "Maybe I can get the invitation before he sees it."

But who do you think was peeking out of the rocks with the invitation in his hand? "Hi, Charlie. Thanks for inviting me to your party."

All week long he sulked. He kicked at his door. "Maybe Sammy will hurt his toe and can't walk."

He picked at his food. "Maybe Skunk will get sick and can't come."

And he sat in the corner and cried. "This will be my worst birthday party ever."

The day of his party, Charlie Chipmunk pulled the covers over his head. "Maybe Sammy Skunk will think my birthday is tomorrow," he wished.

He dilly-dallied putting on his clothes. "Maybe Skink will be late."

But no such luck. When Charlie Chipmunk peeked out of his burrow Oliver Opossum, Robert Rabbit, Billy Beaver, and Sammy Skunk were waiting for them. Opossum was the one who led them in singing HAPPY BIRTHDAY.

"Shhhhh," said Chipmunk. "Loud noises might frighten someone I know."

"Let's play hide and seek," suggested Rabbit.

"No!" cried Chipmunk. "Hiding alone might scare someone I know."

"Can we play catch?' asked Billy. "Is that all right for someone you know."

Charlie looked at Sammy. "I guess that's okay," he said and tossed the ball softly to Skunk. Sammy tossed it to Oliver. They all stood in a circle and tossed the ball around and around.

Soon Opossum stopped.

"Shhhhh," he said. "Do you here what I here?"

"Look!" said Rabbit. "Do you see what I see?"

"Oh no, said beaver. "I see them and here them."

Chipmunk turned around and saw two coyotes running towards them. He heard the coyotes howl, Aaaaar aaaaar

"Help!" squeals Oliver rolling over and playing dead.

"Help!" squeals Robert Rabbit hopping away.

"Help!" squeals Beaver waddling toward the pond. He was scared.

"AAAAAR AAAAAR AAAAAAAAARRRRRRRRRR!"

The coyotes open their mouths and Chipmunk sees their long pointed, sharp, glistening teeth.

"What a birthday," he cried. "We're done for."

Then Charlie Chipmunk heard Skunk hiss. He saw Skunk stamp his feet and raise his tail.

Out it came. Out came Skunk's horrible smell, worse than a rotten egg, worse than a garbage truck, much much worse than anything you've ever smelled before.

"AAAAAAAAAARRRRRRRRRR!"

The coyotes spun around and raced away.

"Yippee! They're gone," whooped Oliver Opossum jumping up.

"Hooray for Skunk!" shouted Rabbit hopping gleefully.

"Three cheers for Skunk!" cried Beaver waddling back.

Charlie Chipmunk hugged Skunk. Thank you. Thank you for saving my birthday."

Then he looked at his friends. Opossum was holding his nose. So were Rabbit and Beaver. Even Skunk was holding his nose.

But not Charlie. He breathed in deeply and smiled.

"You know what Skunk? I'm learning to like your smell."

Then the four friends played more games. The cake was eaten and they watched Charlie Chipmunk open all his presents. Charlie Chipmunk was really sorry to see them leave. Especially he was sorry to see Sammy Skunk go. He realized what a good friend he was.

And he made sure that Sammy came to all his birthday parties from then on.

© Ann Whitford Paul

The more you practice, the more you'll be able to pick out—and avoid—writing errors.

## WHAT'S NEXT?

Your story works now. Not only is the plot compelling, but it's told with tight language that suits the subject matter. Your writing is almost done except for your title. Read on to learn what makes a strong one and some ways to create it.

## BEFORE YOU GO ON

1. Because picture book manuscripts tend to be overly long, cut your story in half. You can go back and add words afterwards. The important thing is to become comfortable writing concisely.

2. If you already write tightly, however, you may need to play around with adding more words. Double your story length. Does it improve your writing? Don't worry. If it feels too long, you can go back and cut.

3. Compare your two versions. What are the strengths and weaknesses? Revise to fit the audience most appropriate for your story.

4. Type up manuscripts of at least five books similar to what you're writing—board book, picture book, or storybook. Compare their word length to yours. Keep these in your computer for easy reference.

5. Read a new picture book.

TYING TOGETHER
LOOSE STORY ENDS

# GRABBING THE READER WITH A GREAT TITLE

 *Many a book is chosen by a reader because
the title seemed promising.* —*Barbara Seuling*

Your picture book is written. You've revised it until it is as close to perfect as possible. You've spent weeks, months, possibly even years getting your manuscript to this point.

Surely now you are done. Finished!

But no! You have to create your title.

Perhaps you already have one. Maybe it came first and was the inspiration for your story. Then you wrote the manuscript. You still like that title. But is it the best it can be?

Blah, boring titles can leave your book on the shelves of stores and libraries, or turn off that all-important editor. The title is the first thing the editor, librarian, or buyer sees. Carol Mann said, "It is a ten-second advertisement." With so many new books published each year, that advertisement better be good.

How hard can coming up with a title be, you ask? Titles are short so they should be easy.

Not so.

The editor Richard Jackson said, "Next to finding a jacket artist, I think titling is the hardest thing to do in children's books."

Editor Reka Simonsen said, "Titles can be a nightmare."

While writing this chapter, I combed the picture books on my shelves. Here are ten titles that jumped out and shouted, "Read me!"

1. ***Click, Clack, Moo: Cows That Type* by Doreen Cronin**. Notice the wonderful consonance of the hard *C*s that telegraph a humorous book. Adults and children will be curious to learn more about cows that know how to type.

2. ***Don't Fidget a Feather!* by Erica Silverman.** I love the word *fidget* and its alliteration with *feather*. Also when anyone says, "Don't," isn't it human nature to want to do the opposite?

3. ***George Washington's Teeth* by Deborah Chandra and Madeleine Comora**. This title lets us know who the book is about. While the subject of our first president is not unusual, the focus on his teeth is new and intriguing. I'm curious to find out more.

4. ***How Much Is a Million?* by David M. Schwartz.** A question is always a come-on for me. Especially this one! How much *is* a million? I have no idea. I want to find out. Notice also the catchy alliteration of *Much* and *Million*.

5. ***How to be a Baby ... by Me, the Big Sister* by Sally Lloyd-Jones**. What a grabbing title! I already know this big sister is bossy and a bit of a know-it-all. I can't wait to read what she's going to say to her younger sibling.

6. **I *Stink!* by Kate and Jim McMullan.** Ohhhhhh! What fun! Children are curious about anything that stinks. Don't they love to go sniffing around, scrunching up their noses at dog poo, baby spit-up, and other smells? The listener doesn't have to see the garbage truck on the front cover to want to pick up this book.

7. ***Muncha! Muncha! Muncha!* by Candace Fleming.** I can tell this book is about eating, but what is eaten and who eats it? The made-up word *Muncha* indicates this will be a silly read. Notice the repetition of three in the title.

8. **Something to Tell the Grandcows by Eileen Spinelli.** That new word, *Grandcows*, catches our attention right off the bat. While kids may not have the knowledge of the phrase "something to tell the grandkids," they still will find the idea of grandcows hilarious.

9. ***That's Good! That's Bad!* by Margery Cuyler.** Okay, I admit it. This is one of my favorite picture books ever, and the title is merely one of the reasons. The repetition of the sentence form is musical, but the words themselves foreshadow a conflict. How can something be good and bad? I have to open the book.

10. ***The True Story of the 3 Little Pigs!* by A. Wolf as told to Jon Scieszka.** This title works for me for the reasons I mentioned in *How to Be a Big Baby ... by Me, the Big Sister.* The teller of the tale, A. Wolf, is obviously going to be feisty, by the use of the word *true*. And doesn't the writer show a sense of humor in the name of the narrator? No wonder this book continues to be so popular.

Do you want to create a title as enticing as these? Then try to include at least one, possibly more, of the following attributes in yours.

# Brief

Not every title can be brief, and some of those listed above are not. However, realize you don't have space on your cover for a long and involved title. The two long titles listed above were on oversized books. Recently at an American Library Association meeting, I wandered the aisles looking at the new books and was surprised to see how brief most of their titles were. Some, like *Olivia*, were just one word.

My first book about patchwork was submitted with the title *Anvil, Buggy Wheel, Churn, Dash* and a subtitle of *A Patchwork ABC*. The art was done and the book was about to be printed when my editor called to say the marketing department needed to shorten the title so it would fit in the index at the back of their catalog. They came up with *Eight Hands Round*. Besides being the name of one of the patterns in the book, it also conjured an image of women working together around a quilting frame. I happily accepted the editor's suggestion.

# Catchy

*The Random House Dictionary of the English Language* defines *catchy* as "pleasing and easily remembered." Pleasing relates to the poetry or musical language of the title, such as *Daddy Is a Doodlebug* by Bruce Degen. The repetition of the letter *D* is certainly musical. It makes the title memorable, along with that word *Doodlebug*.

Another catchy title is *Burgoo Stew* by Susan Patron. The rhyming words are easy to remember.

*River Friendly, River Wild* by Jane Kurtz uses the poetry of repetition to create a memorable title.

# Unique

Titles are not copyrighted, so nothing can stop you from choosing a title for your book that is the same as one of another book. Nothing can stop you, but why would you?

Type in the title *Three Blind Mice* in Amazon.com's search engine and you'll come up with over fifteen hundred hits. Do you want your reader to go through that many books before she finds yours? Would a reader bother to check out that many or would she lose patience and give up entirely on trying to find your book?

Be like Vivian Sathre, who titled her book *Three Kind Mice*. There were seventeen hits for her title, but hers came up first because it was the only one with those exact words.

Research Amazon.com or *Books in Print*, published by R.R. Bowker (available at your library) before you settle on a title. Make sure there aren't hundreds of others like, or close, to yours.

# Straightforward

Don't be too fancy with your title. You may like the sound of the words together, but if they don't reflect what happens in the book, they have to go. I'm not ashamed to say this recently happened to me.

176

My manuscript was about life on the prairie in the 1800s versus life today. I choose the title *Griddle Cakes and Frosted Flakes.* I loved the sound of it. The old-fashioned words vs. the contemporary words indicated the form of the book. I thought I had a winner.

The members of my writing group did *not* think it was a winner. They said it sounded like a breakfast cookbook! Of course, they were correct. The title now, after lots of experimentation, is *Twice Upon the Prairie,* which is a twist on the familiar "Once upon a time" and also accurately says what the book is about. I hope an editor will agree.

Some straightforward titles I love are: *It's My Birthday, Too!* by Lynne Jonell, *Diary of a Worm* by Doreen Cronin, and *The Recess Queen* by Alexis O'Neill. All are clear and concise.

## Expresses the Mood of the Book

Is your book going to be funny or serious, silly or sad? You must get that across in your title. Readers want to know what kind of a story journey they're embarking on. *Can You Make a Piggy Giggle?* by Linda Ashman is not going to be a serious book. Its title brings a smile to the most dour face. *I Will Hold You 'Til You Sleep* by Linda Zuckerman speaks of deep love, rather than a lot of laughs.

## Hints at What the Book Is About

*I.Q. Goes to the Library* by Mary Ann Fraser is not going to be a sports book. Although the title doesn't tell us that I.Q. is a mouse (the illustration does that), we know this is not going to be about music class. *Diary of a Wombat* by Jackie French is not going to be a diary about a kangaroo. *Author: A True Story* by Helen Lester is not about an actress, a baseball player, or a ballerina.

## Doesn't Give Away the Ending

It's easy to fall in love with a last line. That's fine. But don't automatically use it as your title. If Sally Lloyd-Jones had done that, her title would have been *When You Were a Baby* instead of the much more compelling and humorous *How to Be a Baby ... by Me, the Big Sister.*

Even if you don't use your last line, you may still want the reader to know what your book is about. Be careful. Avoid giving away so much information that the reader won't need to pick up your book.

What if Mary Ann Fraser had titled her book *I.Q. Goes to the Library, I.Q. Finds His Funny Book*? The outcome would be obvious. *The Hatmaker's Sign: A Story of Benjamin Franklin,* retold by Candace Fleming, might be titled *The First Is the Best,* but what's the point in reading the stories?

## Creates Suspense

You can do this with a question, which is what Joseph Slate did in *Who Is Coming to Our House?* Or you can title a book like Chris Van Allsburg did simply with *The Stranger.* Who wouldn't be curious to find out who the stranger is? I also am intrigued by Sonia Levitin's title *When Elephant Goes to a Party.* This humorous book shares the proper manners for both an elephant and a child at a party.

## Gives the Artist an Idea for the Cover Illustration

Check out *The Bat Boy & His Violin* by Gavin Curtis. E.B. Lewis illustrated just the title with a batboy holding his violin and the team in muted colors playing behind him. For the title *Do Like a Duck Does!* by Judy Hindley, Ivan Bates painted a fox trying to flap his furry leg wings like the ducklings flap their wings.

## A Child Can Easily Say It Out Loud

It's common sense that if a child is going to ask an adult to read a book, the title has to be something he can say. It shouldn't have too many big words and shouldn't be so long that he'll forget some of the words. My granddaughter used to shorten titles that were too long for her. For a year she called my book *Hello Toes! Hello Feet!* "the foot book." Here are some titles that not even my granddaughter would shorten: *Bugs for Lunch* by Margery Facklam, *Owl Moon* by Jane Yolen, and *Bunny Cakes* by Rosemary Wells.

## Includes the Main Character's Name

Some titles are solely the main character's name, such as *Olivia* by Ian Falconer, *Owen* by Kevin Henkes, and if there is more than one character, *Zelda and Ivy* by Laura McGee Kvasnosky. These titles only work when the character is both strong and distinctive. Usually the characters are illustrated on the cover, and from my small sample of these three titles, the writer and illustrator are often one person.

Other titles include the name and some further information, such as *Ruby the Copycat* by Peggy Rathmann, *Mary Veronica's Egg* by Mary Nethery, and *What's Wrong Now, Millicent?* by Sue Alexander. These titles give us a bit more information about the character and the story.

Obviously, not all titles can contain every attribute mentioned above. But in creating a title you should consider these and see how many yours can include.

How do you create the perfect title?

## Use a Catchy Line From Your Manuscript

Often these lines are repeated several times in the story. Cynthia Rylan's title *When I Was Young in the Mountains* was a phrase used more than once in her book. *If You Want to Find Golden* by Eileen Spinelli uses the repetitive line, "If you want to find ...," mentioning a new color each time and exploring where one might find each different color. April Halprin Wayland's refrain becomes her title in *It's Not My Turn to Look for Grandma!* I did this myself in *If Animals Kissed Good Night.*

The line you choose must be one that also gives the reader a good idea of what the book is about. Comb your manuscript for such a line.

Still nothing?

## Free Association

Write down every title that pops into your mind, referring back to each characteristic of a good title. Free-associate brief titles and then catchy titles, all the way down that list. Don't judge. Some of them will be terrible. Keep on writing and writing until something hits you. You can have pages of possible titles before one works. If nothing strikes a chord, put your list aside and go back to it later. And, if necessary, do it again.

Are you tearing your hair out because you still don't have a title?

## Turn to Outsiders

My writing group has been incredibly helpful with titles. They were the ones who, when I was struggling to come up with something for my prairie book, suggested *Once Upon a Time*, which inspired *Once Upon the Prairie*, which inspired *Twice Upon the Prairie* to pop into my head. Other writers and friends have the advantage of coming to your story fresh. They see things you never noticed and their minds work in different ways than yours. That's why they can bring something new to your search.

Before you settle on a title, remember to go online or check *Books in Print* to make sure there aren't other books with the same title.

We've looked at what makes a good title and how to create a snappy one, but you should know the publisher may change your title for marketing reasons. Feel free to disagree with their decision. Explain why you chose your title and why you think it works better than what your editor suggests. You can even offer alternative titles. However, if your publishing house is unmoving, let it go.

Your book is being published, and you don't want to leave sour feelings with the people who work there. Accept the inevitable, just as you accept that your children will be exposed to ideas, activities, and language that don't please you. This is the way of the world.

Go out and promote your book, no matter what title, as much as you can. The title is a small, albeit important, part of the manuscript. Focus on what's inside the cover, not what is on the cover.

## WHAT'S NEXT?

Now you are convinced you're really done. What possibly could be left? Lucky you! The next chapter is about making a dummy of your story so you can leave your computer again and do some cutting and pasting.

## BEFORE YOU GO ON

1. Think about favorite memorable titles. What makes them stick with you?

2. Using the exercises above, create alternate titles for your story.

3. Select one, then go down the following list and give yourself a happy face, or a star, for each of the characteristics that apply.

    a. Brief
    b. Catchy
    c. Unique
    d. Straightforward
    e. Expresses the mood of your book
    f. Hints at what the book is about
    g. Doesn't give away the ending
    h. Creates suspense
    i. Gives the illustrator an idea for a cover picture
    j. A child can easily say it out loud
    k. Includes the main character's name
       (but doesn't have to)

4. Read a new picture book.

# CUT AND PASTE—
# MAKING A DUMMY BOOK

> *Putting together the ... book dummy is a necessary
> process—it is the foundation for your book and
> lies at the heart of good bookmaking.* —Uri Shulevitz

You've written your story. You've revised the opening until it's tight
and engaging. You've experimented with different ways to tell your
story and chosen the best one. Your characters are strong, unique,
and believable; your plot is a page-turner; and your ending solves
the problem stated in the beginning. You've tied things together so
your audience is satisfied and wants to read or hear the book again.
Your manuscript, whether written in poetry or prose, is poetic.
You've worked to use the right words and you've cut out unnecessary ones. And you've found the perfect title! You should be finished, or ready to share your work with someone else. Perhaps you
think you can skip the sharing step and send it off to a publishing
company right away.

STOP!

YOU'RE NOT DONE YET!

You need to make a dummy.

A dummy is a thirty-two page layout of your text. It's helpful
in determining whether or not the structure of your story fits the
picture book format.

"But I'm not an illustrator," you plead. "I write the words. Illustrators may find making a dummy a positive exercise, but it would be a waste of time for me."

Making a dummy is not only work for an illustrator. A dummy teaches a writer much about her story's strengths and weaknesses.

Trust me on the helpfulness of dummies. For years I tried to get away with not doing them. I was convinced making checkmarks on the hard copy of my manuscript was enough to show me where the page turns came and if I had enough illustration possibilities.

WRONG!

I am one of the converted—a born-again dummy maker.

Today I would never send out a manuscript without first making a dummy. A dummy is a visual and tactile way of evaluating your story.

Most of us who write for children are children at heart. Creating a dummy takes you away from your computer. It gives your back and neck a break. Cutting and pasting allows you to use different hand and arm muscles.

Sometimes, depending on the problems I'm having with a story, I might make several dummies during the writing and revising process. The dummy I make is not one my editor needs to see.

We think of a dummy as the last stage of the revision process. However, it may expose problems that weren't obvious before and may lead to even more revisions and more dummies.

Some writers sketch out a simple, rough dummy early in the writing process or before a word is written. They do this storyboard on a single sheet of paper, dividing it like this into separate pages and spreads.

A spread is two facing pages that end up with an illustration that fills and goes across both of those pages. You can purchase these forms already printed in most art stores. The writer then uses words or phrases here to indicate action, page turns, etc. This is not a dummy with the full text written out. Its purpose is to give you a general overview of the pacing of the story.

The dummy we are going to make now is closer to a finished book with numbered pages you can turn. Print a hard copy of your story, grab some blank paper, tape, and scissors. Here's how it's done.

## THE DUMMY FORM

Staple sixteen pieces of 8½" by 11" paper together along the left side of the papers.

Picture book manuscripts rarely have enough text to fill full pieces of paper. Whenever possible, save a tree and use only eight sheets of 8½" by 11" paper. Cut them in half either vertically (portrait) or horizontally (landscape). You will then have paper measuring either 5½" by 8½" or 11" by 4½". Depending on what side you staple it, your dummy will be long or tall. Choose what dummy shape you want depending on the amount of your text and the line lengths. If your text lines are short, you can have a taller dummy. If they are long, you will make a longer dummy.

You may even have a particularly brief text. Then use just four pages of paper, cut into quarters and staple together.

Now number your pages from 1 to 32. The first is page 1. Turn to the second page and put a 2 on the back of page 1. Number 3 will go on the right-hand page. Continue on until you reach the very back page, which should be number 32.

## CUTTING AND PASTING

Now you're ready to cut and paste sections of your manuscript onto the pages where you think they might go.

In order to do that, you have to consider how many pages will be taken up with **front matter**. This can include four different items.

184

1. **Half-title page.** This usually appears on page 1 and traditionally is the title with only a small illustration.

2. **Full-title page.** This usually appears on pages 2 and 3 and includes not only the title, but also the writer's, illustrator's, and publisher's names.

3. **Copyright information** usually appears on page 4.

4. **Dedications** usually appear on page 5.

On page 6 the story can begin.

Notice, however, the repetition of the words *usually appears*. These days, publishers display a wide range of creativity in the way this front matter is laid out. Page 1 of *Mr. Lincoln's Whiskers* by Karen Winnick contains all the information that would be on the full-title page. The dedication and the copyright information are combined on page 2. On page 3, the story begins.

In *Click, Clack, Moo: Cows That Type,* page 1 is a half title. Page 2 features the dedication and copyright material, and page 3 is the full title with the title again, along with the author's, illustrator's, and publisher's names. The story begins on page 4.

In my book *Hello Toes! Hello Feet!*, page 1 is the half title. Pages 2 and 3 are the full title, and the dedication and copyright material comes on page 32.

Spend time browsing through picture books to see how they present the front matter information.

When you cut and paste your manuscript, plan where that information will go. I usually start pasting my story on page 6. However, if I find I need more pages, I figure out a way to tighten my front matter into a smaller space.

It's time for cutting and pasting. Do not use ordinary tape. You need a lift-off tape (such as Scotch's "Magic" tape). This tape will make it easier for you to shift text from one page to another without tearing your paper.

The hard part is determining where to break up your text. I usually cut when one of the following elements of the story changes.

1. **Location**. Your character leaves the house, enters a store, or goes to a friend's house. The different setting calls for a different picture on a new page.

2. **Characters**. A new character comes on scene or a character disappears. Mother comes home from work, the tooth fairy sneaks into the bedroom, or the cat hides, and the picture can't be the same anymore.

3. **Actions**. What if two characters are fighting, then the fight is broken up? After that, the characters are working together. Each of these would signal a different illustration.

Using your lift-off tape, paste your text on the pages of your dummy. Note that it is not enough to have simple changes in the story. These changes must be dramatic enough to compel your reader to turn the page. Try to leave the odd-number pages with your character in some kind of peril. A classic example of this is Margery Cuyler's *That's Good! That's Bad!* Not every picture book will have such powerful page turns as ten baboons chasing a boy up a tree or the boy discovering the vine he was swinging on wasn't a vine at all but a big, scary snake!

In *Not a Box* by Antoinette Portis, an offstage narrator asks a bunny, "Why are you sitting in a box?" To find out the answer, the reader must turn the page. The book continues with more questions and answers, and readers are eager to see what will come next. An important benefit of making a dummy is to show whether or not you have those necessary page turns.

It will take experimentation and realigning before you are satisfied with where your text works best. That's why you've used the lift-off tape. You can shift your text without ruining the paper in your dummy.

Once your dummy is as complete as you can make it, read it out loud with pen or pencil in hand. The act of reading and turning the pages as your reader will allows you to see the story in a whole new way.

Make necessary changes on your dummy.

That there are always some changes is a constant surprise for me, because I wait to dummy my manuscript until I think my stories are ready to send off. Yet I invariably discover places for revision I hadn't noticed before.

Pay special attention to these questions when evaluating your dummied manuscript.

**1. Does your story fit into a thirty-two page format?** Perhaps your story would work better as a board book. Maybe your story needs forty pages. Beware if you are a first-time writer with a manuscript that needs more than the traditional thirty-two pages. Publishing the book of a new writer is an expensive gamble for a publishing house. Any additional pages might cause an editor to think twice about buying your story.

**2. Does your story have enough illustrations for every page?** The minimum number is thirteen double spreads and one single spread. Thoughts cannot be easily illustrated. The days of bubbles over the heads of characters indicating what's going on in their minds has passed. Some dialogue can be illustrated. "I'm leaving right now" indicates action and could be illustrated with a rabbit leaving her den. "I'm not sure what to do" would be more difficult. Negative statements such as "He didn't jump" or "She didn't read her book" would require great creativity on the part of the illustrator. Don't make her job too challenging. Put action on every page.

**3. Does your text suggest a variety of illustrations?** Does your story take place entirely in one room? While Margaret Wise Brown got away with that in *Goodnight Moon,* give your illustrator a break and vary the illustration possibilities. Give your listener a break, too, so she won't be looking at the same pictures over and over again.

**4. By the first three pages (after front matter), does the reader know what your book is about?** Three pages are generous. All that opening material we discussed in chapter 7 should be on the first page.

**5. Does your story have page turns?** Not every page needs a cliff-hanger, but something should be left unanswered or unfinished to make the reader want to go on.

**6. Is the action spread over thirty-two pages?** Or is it clumped together at the beginning or at the end? This is where you analyze the pacing of your story. Are big chunks of text on some pages and little text on others? Is all of that text important? Can some be deleted?

**7. Are there places you can get rid of unnecessary words?** Look long and hard at clumps of dialogue and description. Can they be tightened? Can they be eliminated? Seeing one's text on the page opens up new possibilities for cutting.

**8. Does your climax happen around page 30 or 31?** If it happens on pages 16 and 17, you have a becuase you'll have to cut much of what follows after. Or you might consider adding more action to the middle of your story.

**9. Do you have a nice tying up of loose ends, on page 32?** We discussed this in detail in chapter 11. With your dummy you'll see how well this works in your story.

**10. Is your story told in the best, most concise, poetic, and dramatic manner?** To answer this question, stop going through your manuscript for the specific attributes of your story. Read your dummy one last time for an overview of how your plot and language work together.

## COLOR TESTING THE DUMMY

After you've made your dummy, get out your highlighters—it's time for more coloring fun.

Use the green highlighter for the *Wow!* moment, where you hope the reader will be compelled to read on. You did this before when we were working on openings, but it's important to repeat here. Turning the pages can show you the *Wow!* moment isn't that much of a *Wow!*

Next use a blue highlighter to show where the problem of the story is revealed. If is doesn't happen within the first three pages of text, some text juggling and cutting is in order.

Using that same blue highlighter, mark the place where the problem is solved. If it comes before pages 28 and 29, more revision is required.

Circle dramatic moments in red. Are there enough? Where did they occur? If they're all close together, or too far apart, can they be moved, expanded, or shortened?

With an ordinary pen or pencil, go through your dummy story again and star places where some question, or drama, creates a page turn. Ideally those should come on every odd-numbered page.

And last of all, the dummy will show if there is a satisfying wrap-up moment on page 32. If you have that, draw yourself a big smiley face.

Here's a sample page of one of my dummies, with corrections and changes for you to see.

"I'll make you fit." Bear pushed on her leg. He prodded. "GRRRRR."

*he*
~~Bear~~ growled. "GRRRRR!"

*clamored*
"It's no use." Biggest-Pie-of-All ~~jumped~~ out of the pan.

"~~Come b~~ack!" Bear lunged at her . . .

This dummy doesn't have to be neat and pretty. It's only for you. Don't send it to an editor. But don't trash it. Save each dummy. Later on, you can compare it to the published book. The layout may be the same or wildly different. That doesn't matter. Just make sure *before* you submit your story to a publishing house that it fits the picture book format.

Don't be a dummy—make a dummy!

## WHAT'S NEXT?

In chapter 18 we'll cover sharing your story with an outside reader. Why must you do this after the many hours and work you've already done? Your story is meant to be read by others. Perhaps others won't see what you are trying to say. Do you want your editor to be the first reader who doesn't get it?

That's why you need to read the next chapter and let someone (maybe several people) read your story.

## BEFORE YOU GO ON

1. Print your manuscript. Dummy it up. Now color test your dummy. Evaluate how well your story works. Play around with the position of text. Revise if necessary.

2. Make dummies of your two published books. Using your highlighter, evaluate each story's strengths and weaknesses. Don't stop with these two texts. Whenever you find a new book you love, type it and print it out. Then make a dummy, study it, and write notes on the pages. It will teach you much about how to create a publishable manuscript. I have a file full of dummies of published picture books.

3. Read a new picture book.

AFTER YOUR STORY IS DONE

# CHAPTER 18

## SHARING YOUR STORY

 *Fine writers should split hairs together, and sit side by side, like friendly apes, to pick the fleas from each other's prose.* —*Logan Pearsall Smith*

I am a firm believer in writing groups. Our picture books are meant to be read by others.

Think of your picture book story as a triangle.

One side is you, the writer. Another side is your words. But it's not a complete triangle until that bottom line, a reader, brings them together.

We want our words to reach and touch both adults and children. We want to share our views and enrich lives. We want to help them through hard times and let them know they're not alone.

If we don't share our work, we'll never know if our words are being received as we intended. Who's better than a group of fellow writers to be your first readers?

A word of warning! Your partner, husband, wife, or parent is *not* a good reader of your manuscript. Neither are your children or your stu-

dents. The best people to read your manuscript are people who also write picture books.

How do you organize a writing group? Read on.

# FINDING MEMBERS

My group evolved from a class I took in picture book writing through UCLA Extension. Several students whose writing I respected joined together to continue meeting after the class ended.

Another writing group I belong to includes members from all over the country. We met in a workshop with Jane Yolen at Centrum (http://centrum.org) in Port Townsend, Washington, and continue to meet yearly to share our works-in-progress. When we're not together, we share manuscripts via e-mail.

Today the Internet is a wonderful place to make contact with other writers who might be willing to critique your work.

However, don't jump eagerly into the first critique group you hear about or that invites you. Choosing a critique group is as important to your work as choosing a mate is important to your life. You hope that your writing group will last forever.

# PERSONAL QUALIFICATIONS

Look for people who share your values about life and about writing.

A writing group, one that endures like mine for over twenty years, evolves into much more than a gathering of professionals. You will discuss your work, and therefore intimate things about yourself, with group memebers … in the same ways you do with your spouse or partner. You need to like these people, to feel safe and unthreatened by them, because they will become your second family—your writing family.

Each member will hopefully grow into a friend. If someone rubs you the wrong way, sends unpleasant vibes, or makes you uncomfortable, don't invite him to be a part of your group.

In your meetings, you will share the frustrations and disappointments of the field. You'll bring rejections and get emotional support. You'll disseminate publishing information. You'll cry when books go out of print and celebrate when stories are accepted and made into books. In my writing group, a sale is marked with champagne and small gifts related to the book.

Friends who don't write can't possibly appreciate the ups and downs of this business like the members of your group. Because they will become such an important part of your life, recognize that adding or subtracting members from an established group can start out smoothly enough but cause an earthquake of changes in the relationships.

But being compatible with your group members isn't everything.

## PROFESSIONAL QUALIFICATIONS

Once I was in a group where the most the other people understood about picture books was that they needed to be short. As you now know, picture books are a unique form and brevity is merely one element. They are a book specialty, the same as orthopedics is a medical specialty. You would never go to an orthopedic surgeon to remove your tonsils. You would not ask your Spanish teacher for help with a math problem. Don't join a writing group that doesn't have members writing what you do. Even people who write children's novels and chapter books aren't able to fully grasp the picture book genre. Please don't make the mistake I did and waste several years sharing manuscripts with people who aren't qualified to comment on them. Surround yourself with picture book writers.

Try to find at least one member of the group who has either published or has more knowledge than you and the others. You will not learn much if you are all beginners. That's like letting first graders teach first graders. Moving ahead would take forever. Find members whose participation will help you grow.

Sometimes you can find a published expert who might require a fee to participate in your group. Pay it. It's money well spent. After a while, you'll learn so much from that person you'll all turn into experts and no longer need to pay anyone.

Make sure you're in a group with writers whose work you respect. Just because a person is published doesn't mean you're bound to like what she writes. If you find yourself in a group with such a person, you might have difficulty accepting her criticism of your work.

Also, don't be in a group where people are not comfortable critiquing. You will get no help from those who only praise your work. Good as it feels at the time, a steady diet of bravos will not help you to publication. Don't tread water in your career. Seek out members who are open, honest, and constructive but not hurtful.

## SIZE

You want your group to be large enough so if one person can't come due to sickness, conflicting events, or simply family and life intrusions, your group will still meet. On the other hand, you don't want a group so big that the critiques will be rushed and some people's work not even looked at because of time constrictions. Three people are in my local group (which is small because one of our members recently died) and seven are in the group with members across the country. The advantage of having more than one group is that after bringing a story to one group several times, the members might lose their objectivity. They will be as close to the story as the writer. A new set of eyes reviewing the work is always beneficial.

## MEETING TIME AND PLACE

Plan a regular schedule for your meetings. This allows everyone to block out their calendars in advance and ensures a professional commitment to one another. How frequently you do that will depend on the availability, writing schedule, and life demands of each member.

Where you meet can vary greatly. Some groups meet in coffee shops, others at the park or the library (that often has rooms available for meetings), or in homes. Sometimes they rotate the homes they meet in; other times they meet at one home. Your group will need to work out those details in a way that is satisfying to all its members.

Some writing groups meet entirely online, sharing manuscripts over the Internet. Often this is just a loose association of people who ask for critiques whenever needed, but it can be scheduled as above.

Let's assume you have your group. You're getting together on a regular basis.

# WHAT HAPPENS IN YOUR MEETINGS?

## Sharing News

Make time for sharing news—both good and bad—and for people to pass along upcoming conference information, good books, and publishing updates. Watch out that the news doesn't last so long it interferes with your critiquing time. Appoint someone as timekeeper who isn't afraid of saying, "Enough! Let's get to work."

An alternative is to share news and business after your critiquing time or perhaps during a food break.

## The Critiquing Process

Since you are a picture book group and your stories are meant to be read aloud, make time to do that. But the story should not be read by the person who wrote it. Why?

The writer knows where the emphasis should be and where the drama is supposed to take place. If the author reads it, the story might sound fabulous but, in fact, need work. The author will not be there to read or explain nuances to an editor or other adult reader.

Much is revealed when you hear another person stumble over a sentence, have difficulty pronouncing words, or deliver the story in a flat and undramatic manner! Hearing a story read out loud will direct the writer to places that need revision.

Some groups have set times for each critique. I have found this to be useless. One manuscript might be almost ready to send out. The changes are small and the discussion brief. Another manuscript may have many areas that require extensive deliberation. Not every manuscript warrents critique for an equal amount of time, but each participant's manuscript should be critiqued with equal interest and attention. Writers learn from every manuscript discussed, not just their own.

# When Your Manuscript Is Being Critiqued ...

During the reading of your story, listen closely to the sound of your words. Pay attention to the other members. Make notes of the places where they look bored, amused, unbelieving, or uninterested.

Then when the comments start, understand this can be an uncomfortable process. You have spilled your blood, sweat, and tears onto the page. You've revised and revised and revised again. Every time I bring a new story to group I am *sure* it's ready to be submitted to an editor. Unhappily, in over twenty years of sharing a new story with my group, I have only heard the words "It's wonderful, send it off" once. I'm sorry to say that story has not yet sold. Maybe it wasn't so ready after all.

Getting one's fantasies squashed is hurtful. No one likes hearing that your baby isn't ready for delivery to the world. But don't think you're the only one who's uncomfortable about sharing. Everyone is, especially in the beginning.

The good news is that after many times of critiquing with others, your discomfort will abate. You will understand the others are not criticizing you as a person. They are attempting to help make your manuscript the best it can be. You will learn to be grateful for their honesty and constructive comments and will look forward to sharing your writing.

When the comments start coming, zip up your mouth unless you are asked a direct question. Take notes on what you hear; don't argue, "But this really did happen!"

Do not question, "Why would you think that?"

Do not defend, "My husband loved that part."

Your job is to *listen* to the criticism. Take it in. Write it down. Make notes as necessary. Later, when everyone is finished, you may ask your questions. "What did you mean when you said the character was too passive? How could I tighten my opening? Why wasn't my ending strong?"

Now is also the time to say, "You're taking my story in a new direction. What I want my story to say is ... (you fill in the blank). Why is what I want to say not coming across clearly? How can I change my writing to make it in tune with my theme?"

Then go home with your notes and consider the comments carefully. You may find yourself feeling exhilarated after your meeting because your story needs few changes before it's ready to be sent out.

Or you may not feel exhilarated, but at least comfortable with the direction you need to go. Perhaps the suggestions were ones you agreed with. Making them will be work, but not a burden. I try to do this kind of revision within a day or two of our meeting so the comments are still fresh and I can remember what my shorthand stands for.

Must you make all the changes your group suggests?

Absolutely not.

Each comment is merely an opinion. Some of these comments will feel wrong, and you can discard them immediately. Some comments you may not be so sure about. They may improve your story or they may not. The only way you can find out is to try them. If they're a disaster, you can go back to your original. Some comments are so right-on you make the changes immediately.

Be forewarned—it's not enough to make one change and forget about the rest of the manuscript. Every change, no matter how small, has ramifications that impact your entire text. Don't assume that one change solves the problem. It usually creates inconsistencies elsewhere in your manuscript. Don't rush your revisions. Watch for unexpected impact throughout.

You may need to take your manuscript back to your group several, perhaps even many, times before you feel confident it's ready to send to an editor. If your group works with your story many times, it's possible they will become so connected to it that they, like you, may lose objectivity.

Then you need to do one of two things—show it to another writer or another group, or put it aside for several weeks or months, however long it takes, before bringing it back to your group.

Sadly, after your critique you may not feel exhilarated or comfortable with your group's comments. You may leave the meeting discouraged and depressed. Your story isn't reaching the reader the way you hoped. The ideas thrown out by your group don't sit right with you. You have to go back to the drawing board and rethink everything. This can feel like a Herculean task.

If you think you can push forward immediately, do. But if you're not up to it, put your story away, let it sit on the back shelf, and see if while you're going about your life your creative mind can come up with a solution.

Be willing to accept that some stories won't ever work and move on. Giving up on a project is not a sign of failure. It's a sign of strength not to pound your head against a cement wall. And it's a sign of strength to say, "I've learned everything I can from this story. I'm ready to apply those lessons to my next project."

## When You Are Doing the Critiquing ...

It works best, especially in the early time of your group's life, to begin with positive comments.

The positive can be as general as "I like the message you're trying to get across." Or "You've worked really hard on this revision." And then go on to make your comments. Avoid general comments like "I like this a lot." That is not specific enough to be helpful. Let the writer know what works for you, such as "I like the way your character steps in and takes action" or "Your opening is strong. You dropped me right into the action."

Focusing your comments will help the writer whose manuscript is being critiqued and will also help others see how important it is for the main character to take action or to understand what makes a strong opening. Specificity allows everyone to learn from the manuscript.

Suppose there are no positives?

My answer is: not possible.

Every manuscript, no matter how bad, comes from a place deep within the writer. Respect that. You might begin by asking the writer what he is trying to say.

If you hate the manuscript, bite your tongue. Focus on specific parts in the story that didn't work for you. "I found it hard to believe the voice of your main character. You say he's six years old, but he speaks like an adult" or "Perhaps you have too much setup in the beginning. I wonder if the real opening comes in the first paragraph of your second page." By pointing to the exact places that don't work, you are giving specific information to the writer about where and why the story doesn't work.

In critiquing, refrain from relating personal experiences. The focus here must be on the story, not on the remembrances or connections it makes for you. Personal stories waste valuable critiquing time.

Divide your critiques into three areas.

199

## Big Issues

Start with major questions about how the story is working.

1. What is the writer trying to say? Is it more than an incident? Does the main character change or learn something new at the end?

2. Is the main character a child or childlike? Are there superfluous characters who don't move the story forward?

3. Is it really a board book? Picture book? Picture storybook? Would this story be better told as a chapter book or an early reader?

4. Does the story have more than one level? Does it say something? Does it have depth?

5. Is the story new and unique? Is the idea old or overdone? How might the writer bring freshness to it?

6. Is the story tightly focused? Is it about one thing or one aspect of a thing?

When all of these questions have been answered satisfactorily, you can move on.

## Middling Issues of Form and Structure

1. Is the opening strong and compelling? Has the setup and description gone on too long?

2. Does the plot build to a pivotal point or climax?

3. Does the ending grow out of the story? Does it evoke an emotional response and make the reader want to read again?

4. How well does the story fit the thirty-two-page format? Look at the dummy.

   a. Does the problem become clear by the third spread (at the latest)?

b. Are there strong page turns?

c. Does the resolution come on pages 30 or 31, or at least close to the end?

d. What about picture variety?

e. Is there a nice twist, punch line, or satisfying *ah ha* moment on page 32?

5. Does the language fit the story?

6. Does the writer milk the emotion with cadence, rhythm, and the tools of poetry, alliteration, consonance, assonance, etc.?

7. Do the characters speak appropriately?

8. How can this story be best told? In verse or no verse?

## Fine-Tuning

It's wasted time to focus on this too early because the story may change completely. Only consider the smaller issues of grammar and tight writing after everything discussed above is resolved.

1. Is the writer using too many passive, instead of active, verbs?

2. Does the writer tell, rather than show?

3. Are there excess words that don't move the story forward?

a. Qualifying words (*almost, nearly, seemed like,* etc.)

b. Adjectives and adverbs (find the strong verb that says it all)

c. Action details that don't move the story forward

d. Purple prose

e. Attributions of dialogue (said and action)

Because you've read this book and done the activities in the chapters, you will come to a critique with another writer or a group a step ahead of the others. You know what's important and how to take and give criticism.

I would not be the writer I am today without my critique groups. While I have improved on the versions I first bring them and the process of revising moves faster, I still could not write without them.

Unfortunately not all critique groups survive. Sometimes they die a natural death as members move away or stop writing, or maybe the personalities don't mesh.

Then end your participation and find another, more helpful group. Don't be afraid to say good-bye. Create a new writing family.

## WHAT'S NEXT?

After you've shared your story, you really are done. In chapter 19 we're going to explore the submission process and how to find the right publisher for your book.

## BEFORE YOU GO ON

1. Share your story with another writer or with a writing group.

2. Revise if necessary.

3. If indicated, repeat above steps 1 and 2 until you and your group feel the story is the best it can be.

4. Read a new picture book.

# BECOMING A DETECTIVE—
# RESEARCHING THE MARKET

*You know how it is in the kid's book world:*
*It's just bunny eat bunny.* —*Anonymous*

You've done it! You've written a fabulous story and spent hours, days, weeks, even months or years, revising it. You're confident, and your writing group agrees it will make a fabulous book.

Larry Dane Brimner said, "No manuscript was ever published sitting in a drawer." Nor, I would add, hidden in a file in your computer.

It's time to muster your courage and send it out into the big wide world.

But first you have to find the right publisher for your book. What a shame it would be to waste your hard work by sending your story out pell-mell to any and all publishers in the country!

You need to have a plan, and that means you still have work to do. But this will be different. It will get your numb bun out of your writing chair and your blurry eyes away from your computer screen.

## THE FIRST STEP IS TO FIND
## THE RIGHT PUBLISHER

The variety of publishers is almost beyond counting. Some publishers do only adult books. Some are further specialized under the adult category, publishing only cookbooks, historical books, romance novels,

nonfiction, or how-to books. Immediately cross off all those who publish nothing but adult books. You may think your manuscript is so brilliant everyone will jump at it. Not so! Even if an adult publishing company were to publish it, they would not have the sales and marketing departments to get your book into the hands of your specific audience.

You want a children's book publisher, and not just any children's book publisher.

# A PICTURE BOOK PUBLISHER

Many publishers focus on chapter books or novels.

But a publisher of picture books still has room for more specificity. You want a publishing house that publishes *your* kind of picture book. Suppose your picture book has the potential for distinctive and detailed art. Then you'd look for a publisher who does lovely art books, not a publisher whose books are mostly illustrated with simple line drawings.

If you've written a fictional picture book, you wouldn't send your manuscript to a publisher who only works with nonfiction manuscripts.

Finding the right publisher for your book requires a new workplace—the library or a bookstore. Walk, ride, bike, or drive to the nearest one and page through as many picture books as you can. Make a list of the publishing houses of the books you like and respect. Write the titles of those books next to the name of the house for future reference.

Watch out for published books that are too similar to yours. If one publishing house has had great success with a book about a pig with illustrations that fit your image of your pig story, hold back! Don't send your manuscript there. Chances are they won't want another book of a similar vein on their list. However, if you've written a funny book about a pig and you find a house that publishes lots of funny books, you might put that name on the top of your list for submissions.

Unless a book is dedicated to the editor or is under a specific editor's imprint, you won't be able to glean the name of the person who worked on the book. Sometimes a call to the publishing office's front desk can reveal that information, but some publishers don't share that knowledge. You may have to contact other writing acquaintances to get the scoop. If you're not a member of the Society of Children's Book Writers and Illustrators, now is the time to join. Check out their Web site at www.scbwi.org. They update their *Market Survey: Publishers of Books for Young People* every August with publishers' areas of focus and names of their editors. They also make available to members a list of editors and the books they've edited, titled *Edited By ....*

Writer's Digest publishes a yearly update of markets for children's stories in their *Children's Writer's & Illustrator's Market*. It's packed with up-to-date information on publishing houses, including names of editors, whether or not they're taking unsolicited submissions, and their loves and hates in manuscripts. *CWIM* also includes a section of literary agents who handle children's material. You'll find this book in libraries, bookstores, or online.

Another resource, *Children's Writer*, is a monthly newsletter containing a section titled "Marketplace" that provides the latest information concerning publishers' wants and needs. You can access it online at www.childrenswriter.com.

Another way to get information is through your contact with other writers. But suppose there aren't any other children's writers nearby. You're only a click of your mouse away from a community of writers more than willing to share their knowledge about publishing.

Search for children's writers in Yahoo! groups and see if there's a group you'd like to join. While you're on the Internet, check out each publisher's Web site. Peruse their catalog and even look inside some of the books. If you are old-fashioned, write to the publishing house and ask for one of their catalogs to page through at your leisure.

With so much up-to-date facts and communication available, there's no excuse for getting back a manuscript with this note: *Sorry, we don't publish picture books.* You should have known that in advance. Think of the postage you could have saved and all the time and emotional energy you wasted waiting for a reply.

In any business, personal contacts mean a lot. Therefore, go to every writing conference you can, especially those with editors in attendance. You'll learn a great deal about the different publishing houses and also discover which editors you find the most compatible.

If part of the conference program includes an opportunity to submit a manuscript for critique, do it. You might be lucky enough to get an editor or an agent to read your manuscript. The editor might even like your manuscript and buy it! An agent might offer to represent you. (You'll find my thoughts on agents later in this chapter.) Organizers of a conference like nothing better than to be able to announce the sale of a manuscript.

But suppose you don't sell your manuscript or find an agent. All isn't lost. A good friend was once given great suggestions from an editor for revisions. She did revise and ... Happy Ending! ... the editor later bought the story.

Maybe your manuscript won't be assigned to an editor. Still, there's hope. At the SCBWI Annual Summer Conference in Los Angeles (held every August), the writers, agents, editors, etc. who critique are allowed to submit one manuscript for the Sue Alexander award—a trip to New York and meetings with editors.

And even if your story doesn't merit any of the above, you still go out a winner because you received additional feedback on your story from a publishing professional or a knowledgeable author.

At most conferences, the editors in attendance offer to read manuscripts from the attendees, even if their company doesn't normally take unsolicited manuscripts. If you like the editor and the picture books her house publishes, submit your story to her.

Try not to be too shy at conferences. This advice is coming from a writer who would rather fade into the wallpaper than approach an editor about a project, so do as I say, *not* as I do.

Tell yourself editors are people just like you. Some of them are shy, too, and insecure. If you honestly liked an editor's talk, by all means go up and introduce yourself, or send her an e-mail or snail-mail note telling her so. If you have a project you think would be just what she's looking for, tell her about it. An editor's job depends on discovering the next great book. Perhaps that next great book will be yours.

The bigger the community of writing friends, the bigger will be the reach of your information network. Obviously we don't become friends with other writers just to pick their brains, but true friendship includes sharing publishing news. Children's writers are especially generous when it comes to that.

## MAKING SENSE OF PUBLISHERS' SUBMISSION POLICIES

Some publishers will only read exclusive manuscripts, those submitted to just one publishing house at a time. Other publishers, understanding how long it can take for a manuscript to be evaluated, will accept manuscripts you've sent to other houses (called simultaneous submission) if you tell them. Be sure you know what each house prefers.

Some publishers will only look at manuscripts submitted by an agent. You don't have an agent? No problem. Many of those houses will accept a query letter about your story. Make it lively and intriguing and they may ask to see it. Or they may not.

It's not the end of the world. By this time you should have a list of more than one publisher who might be right for your story. Cross off any publisher that doesn't take unsolicited manuscripts. Tell yourself it's their loss, and go on to the next house on your list.

I do not have an agent and have found, in going over my SCBWI *Market Survey*, that about half of the publishing houses still take unsolicited manuscripts. Those houses, in addition to editors I've met at conferences and workshops, give me plenty of places to send my stories.

Some publishers have specifications about the manner in which your manuscript may be submitted. They will not consider a manuscript sent via fax or e-mail. Other publishers want submissions only that way. Some publishers, if a self-addressed, stamped envelope, or SASE, is enclosed will return a manuscript they're not interested in. Other publishers won't return your manuscript but will shred it instead. Some publishers say if you haven't heard from them in six months, they're not interested in your story. Make sure you understand each house's submission and return policies before sending out your story.

Your submission should include the following items.

# Cover Letter

Here's a sample.

Ima Insecure Writer
777 Rejection Street
Nowhere, California 90027
phone (333) 661-HELP, fax (333) 6-PLEASE
e-mail Tryingagain@unpublished.com
May 7, 2009

Ms. Wonderful Editor
Best Publishing House
1234 Fifth Street
New York, NY 10000

Dear Ms. Editor,

Enclosed is a manuscript for a picture book titled *Ready for Publication*. I am familiar with many of the fine books you publish. *Not Another Rejection* is one of my favorite books. Yours is a list I would be proud to be a part of.

The idea for this story came to me after taking numerous classes in writing. I read many books and interviewed other unpublished authors. There is no picture book in print on this subject.

I became interested in writing children's stories after years of bedtime reading to my own four children. I have sold stories (one of them won an award) to *Highlights* and *The Friend*. In addition, several of my articles have appeared in *The Los Angeles Times* and *The San Diego Union*. I am a member of the Society of Children's Book Writers & Illustrators.

I hope you will find *Ready for Publication* worth adding to your list and look forward to hearing from you. An SASE is enclosed for your convenience.

Yours truly,

Ima Insecure Writer

While this letter is silly, it includes important elements that should be part of every cover letter.

**1. Brevity.** Don't weary an editor with too much writing. One page is plenty. The editor wants to get to your manuscript. Help him get there quickly.

**2. Compliments.** Editors like them just as much as we do. If you honestly admire a book they've edited, mention it.

**3. No description of your story.** Let your manuscript speak for itself. However, you might mention how you got the idea, along with any expertise you have on the subject and research you've done.

**4. Publishing credits.** Don't worry if you don't have any. Every writer has to start somewhere. However, if you have them, state them. If you can't do it briefly, attach a sheet so the editor doesn't have to plod through them in the letter. I have bookmarks printed with all my books to stick into the envelope along with my cover letter and manuscript.

## Manuscript

Use a simple, black, clear 12-point font. Include a title page that looks like the example on the following page.

**IF ANIMALS KISSED GOOD NIGHT ...**

By

Ann Whitford Paul

Ann Whitford Paul
456 North Main Street
Los Angeles, CA 90027
phone 555 987-6543
fax 555 987-6543
e-mail ann@annewhifordpaul.net
Web site www.annwhitforpaul.com

The title, followed by the author's name (I use three spaces between each line) goes midway down the page and is centered. In the bottom right-hand corner place your contact information.

The first page of your manuscript should look like this:

Ann Whitford Paul
456 North Main Street
Los Angeles, CA 90027
phone 555 987-6543
fax 555 987-6543
e-mail ann@annewhifordpaul.net
Web site www.annwhitforpaul.com

**IF ANIMALS KISSED GOOD NIGHT ...**

If animals kissed

like we kiss good night,

Sloth and her cub

in late afternoon's light

would hang from a tree

and start kissing soooooo sloooowwwwwww ...,

the sky would turn pink

and the sun sink down low.

Peacock and chick

On this first page, repeat the contact information in the upper left-hand corner and start the story halfway down the page. Type in your title and then three double-space skips before you start the manuscript. Keep 1-inch margins on all sides, except at the top, where I use only half an inch. You will understand why when you look at the second page.

Ann Whitford Paul  2
IF ANIMALS KISSED GOOD NIGHT ...

spin a fan dance
and kiss with a kickity
high-stepping prance.
Mama Python and hatchling
would kiss waggling around,
twirling and twisting
like rope loosely wound.
Walrus calf and her papa
would make whiskery swishes,
rubbing each other
in scritch-scratchy kisses.
Mama Elephant's trunk
would kiss and then sway
and shower her calf
with a wet, washy spray.
 If animals kissed
 like we kiss good night,
 the sky would turn dull,
 the moon a chalk white—

Do you see the header at the top of the page, with the writer's name and the title of the manuscript on the left side (facing you) and the page number on the right side (facing you)? These are usually single-spaced along with four more single spaces before the text starts. These headers should be on every page of your manuscript, and succeeding pages should look identical to this. The only difference will be with your last line. After that, double-space and make a line of asterisks so the editor will know the story is over like this:

> kissing good night!

★★★★★★★★★★★★★★★★★★★★★★★★★★★★★★★★★★★★★★★★★★★★★★★★

Please note this manuscript was a poem and therefore submitted in poetic line lengths. A prose story would have normal paragraphs without extra spaces for paragraphs or to indicate a page turn.

If you are unsure about punctuation or paragraphing, grammar, or any other nitpicky detail, refer to a grammar book for professional advice before submitting your story. Carefully check your manuscript for spelling errors. It's not enough to spell-check with your computer. That handy convenience will not pick up when you use the word *sew* for *so* or *there* for *their*. Slowly read your manuscript out loud. It's the only way to catch those mistakes.

## Self-Addressed Stamped Envelope

Include one only if the publisher requests it.

Now you're ready to send out your manuscript.

# HOW TO FIND AN AGENT

If I had a dollar for every time I've been asked how to connect with an agent, I'd be rich. The problem comes because the most important question is not how to get an agent but how to write a strong, salable story.

But if you've already written that strong, salable story, the question is valid.

I have worked with and without agents, and I've sold stories both ways.

While it's difficult, it's not impossible to get an agent before you sell your first story. The problem is: Agents can reject you as easily as an

213

editor. Agents usually ask for the same things as a publishing house—a cover letter about why you're contacting them, a copy of the manuscript (perhaps more than one) you'd like them to sell. They, too, can take months to get back to you.

My personal feeling is to sell your first story on your own. Then you can go to the agent with a track record.

Another problem is that many children's book agents aren't thrilled to take on a writer of picture books. If the agent sells your story, the advance must be split between the writer and the illustrator. Your royalty (if you're the writer only) is usually a whopping 5 percent of the list price—not enough to pay the water bill unless you sell millions of copies or publish several stories a year.

Most writers, besides having an agent to submit their manuscripts, want him to deal with money issues. Some agents are very good at negotiating deals. If your advance doesn't arrive in a timely fashion, your agent can nudge the publisher into action. If there's any working problem between you and the editor, the agent can smooth things over.

However, if you're not shy, you can deal with all these things. A former editor told me that publishers never come in with their best offer. They expect to dicker and they leave room in for dickering. You'd be foolish not to try for more.

Confession time!

I was a fool with my first two contracts. It didn't matter with my first book, but an escalation clause for my second book, which would have upped my royalty percentage as the sales increased, did matter a lot. That book has sold 100,000 copies, and I'd be richer if I'd asked for that escalation clause.

This probably sounds like gobbledygook to you, but there's help. If you're a member of The Authors Guild (www.authorsguild.org), they have lawyers who will go over your contracts with you. One of the numerous benefits of belonging to the Society of Children's Book Writers & Illustrators is a sample children's book contract you can download from their Web site (www.scbwi.org).

If you've decided you want an agent, you must research. Introduce yourself to agents at conferences. Talk to established writers. Find out whom they recommend and whom they stay away from. Talk to your editor about agents she likes working with. Look online. Speak with the agent. Do you feel compatible?

Having an agent is almost like being married. There will be moments of frustration and moments of true affection. You wouldn't settle for a life partner; don't settle for an agent who doesn't believe in you and your work and with whom you can have a comfortable working relationship.

# REJECTIONS

You may be one of the lucky few who sells your story the first time out.

Unfortunately, most manuscripts are returned, often with nothing more than a form rejection addressed *Dear Author.*

To say it's discouraging is an understatement, especially since some of us let our minds run wild while we're waiting to hear from the publishing house. Like Walter Mitty, I dream an editor will buy my story the day she receives it and call to rave about how the book will turn me into the new Dr. Seuss.

That never happens.

So how do you deal with the disappointment?

Remind yourself of what novelist Jane Smiley said: "Rejections are business letters, not personal letters."

When I was first writing and deep into raising four children, I looked at rejection letters as contact with the adult outside world. I told myself, at least I was in the game.

Another way of dealing with disappointment is to put on your boxing gloves and leap back into the ring. Tell yourself the publishing house that rejected you will be sorry because you'll sell the story to someone else. They'll watch it win many awards and appear on numerous top ten lists and they'll groan, "Why did we ever reject that story?"

That probably won't happen either, but it's important not to allow a stranger to affect your confidence in your work.

Some stories are rejected for reasons that have nothing to do with the quality of writing. Perhaps the reader who opened your manuscript about the death of a dog had just put her dog to sleep and couldn't bear to go on past the first line. The rejection is not always about your writing. The publishing house may already have a similar book. Or they've decided to cut back on the number of picture books published, as many are doing at the time of this writing. Don't panic. Not long ago, editors at conferences stated emphatically, "Don't send fantasy" or "Young adult books are dead." And then came Harry Potter. If the pendulum is swinging away from picture books, be confident that soon it will swing back. Use your time while waiting to keep writing and honing your craft.

Walter Davenport said, "An editor is a person who knows precisely what he wants but isn't quite sure."

Different people respond to different movies, different editors respond to different books. Perhaps the editor wasn't the right one for your project.

If a book has been rejected with a form letter more than half a dozen times, you might want to put it on the back burner for a while or at least look at it again and make sure it's the best you can do. You might even take it back to your writing group.

That time away from your story while it's circulating can give you the necessary distance you need to be able to see it with a fresh eye.

You may get a personal note from the editor at the publishing house. It can be a brief personal note and maybe even contain suggestions for revisions.

Jean Cocteau said, "Listen carefully to first criticisms of your work. Note just what it is about your work that the critics don't like—then cultivate it. That's the part of your work that's individual and worth keeping."

This quote meant a lot to me when I received rejection letters criticizing the quietness of my stories. Of course my stories were quiet. I was inspired to write after years of bedtime reading to my four children. I wanted to create stories adults and children could share together before a nap or bedtime.

However, that quietness had to be addressed. I had to learn ways to add tension to every story, no matter how peaceful.

If you get suggestions for revisions and they feel right to you, do them. But don't rush. Even the smallest revisions can ripple through your manuscript and require tumultuous changes. Take your time. If you're worried the editor might forget your manuscript, relax. Remind him of his previous letter, perhaps including a copy of it when you resubmit.

If an editor's suggestions feel off base, put the manuscript and the letter away for a while. Getting rid of your disappointment is the first step to reading the editor's comments without emotion. It brings your professionalism to the front and might even allow you to consider that the editor may be right. But if after some time you still don't agree, and you feel confident in your story, submit it elsewhere.

Let's close with ten commandments for submitting picture book manuscripts.

1. Thou shalt only send out your best work.

2. Thou shalt inform all publishers if you are making a multiple submission.

3. Thou shalt immediately inform the other publishing houses if and when your manuscript has sold.

4. Thou shalt submit all manuscripts via US Postal Service unless otherwise requested by an editor. Do not hand a manuscript to an editor at a conference and expect an immediate response.

5. Thou shalt not skip spaces to show page turns, nor put in parentheses picture descriptions, nor use fancy fonts or colored inks.

6. Thou shalt not submit your manuscript with illustrations unless *you* are the illustrator or unless you state in your cover letter that you are willing to sell your story without the illustrations and vice versa.

7. If your manuscript comes back with a personal rejection letter or a note on a form rejection, thou shalt immediately write a thank-you to the editor. Thou shalt consider any suggestions seriously. If you still believe in your manuscript, thou shalt promptly send it out again.

8. If after four months you have not heard from the publishing house, a letter of inquiry is acceptable. Be sure to

include an SASE, or postcard, for their answer. If after six months you have still not heard from the publishing house, thou shalt inform the publisher you are submitting your story elsewhere.

9. Thou shalt remember that a rejection of your manuscript is not a rejection of you. It is merely a business letter and signifies that thou art a professional writer who actively submits your work.

10. Thou shalt *never* give up on a story, or on your chosen career of writing picture books, after one rejection.

## WHAT'S NEXT?

Now you know the form of submissions and how to find the right publishing house and agent. You've also learned how to deal with rejections. Chapter 20 is about what to do after you've sent off your manuscript.

## BEFORE YOU GO ON

1. Go to your library or children's bookstore and research different publishers. Rank six publishers in order of preference. Check out their submission requirements.

2. Submit your story.

3. If it comes back after these six with form rejections, revise or put it away for a while.

4. Read a new picture book.

# PRIMING YOUR
# IDEA PUMP

 *A productive writer learns that you can't
wait for inspiration.* —Susan Sontag

You've finished your manuscript. You've sent it off to a publishing house with high hopes for acceptance. Now what do you do?

    a. Mope around and worry it might get lost in the mail?
    b. Rewrite your story over and over again in your mind?
    c. Take a vacation from writing?
    d. None of the above?

If you answered d, you are correct.

Get back to work.

The best way to make time pass while waiting to hear the editor's response is to jump into another project.

Don't say, "It's too hard."

Quit saying, "I don't have any good ideas."

Don't think, "If I can just sell my manuscript, I'll have the confidence to write another."

As my grandfather would have said, "Hogwash!"

First of all, let's be honest. Your manuscript probably won't sell the first time out ... or, I'm sad to say, the second or the third or maybe even the tenth. No matter how much you have revised and polished, it would be a minor miracle if an editor bought the story right away.

I recently heard author Tod Goldberg say, "If a writer's sales to manuscripts submitted were calculated like a baseball player hitting a ball compared to times at bat, we writers would look pretty pathetic." A baseball star like Barry Bonds, the home run king, hit over .330, or one-third of his times at bat. A writer, on the other hand, would be a star with a selling average of .150, or selling a little over one out of ten times submitted. So you can see the odds aren't good.

Five years passed and 180 not-interesteds arrived in my mailbox before I sold my first manuscript. I'm not trying to discourage you. I want to *encourage* you. The struggle, work, and rejections are all part of the dues one has to pay to enter the published-author club. You may get admitted earlier than I did. Maybe later, but if your passion is there and you are temporarily depressed, know you are not the only one who receives bad news from a publishing house.

But there is a way to improve your odds of selling a manuscript.

1. Write more stories.
2. Revise each story to the best of your ability.
3. Submit your story to a publisher you've researched and know is looking to do your kind of book.

We've already covered steps 2 and 3. This chapter is about the first step—writing more stories.

But your mind is blank. You're exhausted from many hours and multiple revisions on your last story. You'd prefer to sit awhile, thank you very much, and bask in the warm feelings of completing and submitting your manuscript.

Don't!

Sit down with a new idea and start writing. The time waiting to hear from an editor will pass more quickly, and the mail carrier will appreciate your not standing by the door each day pathetically asking, "Anything from my publisher yet?"

But how do you get a new idea?

Where does inspiration come from?

I was a very insecure writer (I still am), but I used to be especially insecure about ideas. It seemed other writers came up with the most wonderful, zany ideas, but mine were flat and boring.

There are two schools of thought about getting ideas.

James Dickey, poet and novelist, wrote: "A poet is someone who stands outside in the rain hoping to get struck by lightning."

This may work for him and for other writers, but personally the idea of getting soaked until lightning strikes is not appealing.

I'm more of a Jack London kind of writer, who said: "You can't wait for inspiration. You have to go after it with a club ..." or, as I would put it, *with a pump.*

Years ago, my favorite task when visiting my grandparents' farm was to bring up water from the outdoor well, though it was not necessary since they had modernized the house with indoor plumbing. All one needed to do was turn on the spigot and water spewed out. Still, I preferred to do it the old-fashioned way.

That was more of a challenge. It took several steps.

First I had to pour a pitcher of water from the kitchen sink to prime the pump. Then I had to lift the pump's handle up and push it down, up and down, up and down, until my arms ached. Just when I thought I couldn't do it one more time, cold, clear water splattered into my pail and onto my legs and feet.

That's a water pump. The pump needed help to bring up the water, just as we need help getting ideas. How do you prime your writing pump?

Several years ago a tomato plant sprouted in the middle of my flower garden. My husband and I spent lots of time discussing how the plant might have gotten there.

Did the tomato plant come from a seed floating in the air?

Did someone, or some animal, plant the tomato seed there?

Did I plant it there and not remember?

Was the seed hidden in the earth and only after much time reached the surface?

Why, you're wondering, am I talking about inspiration and a tomato plant in the same breath? Because the different ways seeds and ideas arrive have lots in common.

Let's consider how to start the creative juices running in your writing pump.

# Writing Ideas, Like Tomato Seeds, Are Floating in the Air

They're everywhere, waiting for us to grab them and plant them in our brains. Find them by paying close attention to the world around you.

**Look at your newspaper**, not just to read the news, but to find something that might spark a story. Yesterday *The New York Times* had an article about helping children in New Orleans through art therapy. Instead of drawing the usual house—a square with two windows and a door and a peaked roof—after Hurricane Katrina, children drew houses that were mere triangles.

What could that mean?

When you read an article, take time to let your mind wander through several story possibilities.

Could I write about a child surviving Katrina?

Or another disaster? We were close to being evacuated recently due to a wildfire. Maybe I should write about it.

Or I could write about a child who loves to draw, or hates to draw, or better yet, is afraid to draw.

**Pictures in a magazine** can start story juices running. I love pictures of children, but even a picture of a snow-covered mountain can get me writing. The key is to use the article or picture as a kickoff. Let your free-association thoughts lead you to the story idea that strikes your fancy.

Still no story?

Don't give up. Remember how much you loved *Goldilocks and the Three Bears* or perhaps *The Little Red Hen*? **Rewrite a classic children's story** in a different location, or change the time period, or even turn the female characters into males. Helen Ketteman changed Cinderella into a cowboy and wrote a hit, *Bubba the Cowboy Prince: A Fractured Texas Tale*.

**A change of scenery can stimulate an idea.** Get up from your desk. Go for a walk. My book *Hello Toes! Hello Feet!* came to me while on a stroll around the block. I was frustrated with revisions for another story and needed to get away from my computer. I began to think about what I walked on—my feet—and had completed the first draft in my head by the time I returned home.

**Go to the zoo.** Pick out a favorite animal. Then give that animal an ability that it couldn't possibly have in the real word. Ask yourself the *What if?* question. Remember how Dumbo the elephant could fly? You could write about an alligator who can't swim. Or a giraffe whose neck is short. Or a hippopotamus who hated vegetables. Come up with your own *What ifs?* Perhaps you'll create a story from it.

While you're at the zoo, linger close to a group of kids and listen to them talk. Of course, you can eavesdrop on children anywhere ... at the mall, a playground, a restaurant, just walking down the street. I once wrote a story, still unpublished, inspired by a little boy I overheard asking his mother, "Will my baby sister grow up to be six?"

## Your Writing Idea, or Tomato Seed, Might Have Been Planted by Someone Else

Ask someone to give you an assignment.

Ask me!

Here's your assignment: A child opens a suitcase and takes something out. What did she/he take out? Why? Make up a story about it.

Here's another assignment. Write a story about a rabbit and a bear. I guarantee even if every person who reads this book writes a story about a rabbit and a bear, each one will be different. You have your own style, your own voice, your own background, and your own idea of plotting.

Want another assignment?

Check out these books:

- *Poemcrazy: Freeing Your Life With Words* by Susan Goldsmith Wooldridge

- *Story Sparkers: A Creativity Guide for Children's Writers* by Debbie Dadey and Marcia Thornton Jones

- *I'd Rather be Writing* by Marcia Golub

They and other books on your library or bookstore shelves are full of assignments to get creative juices up and running.

Ask a friend or your writing group to give you a topic to write about.

# You Planted Your Own Writing Idea or Tomato Seed

Give yourself a writing assignment. These are the two writing assignments I often give myself.

First of all, I open a children's dictionary at random. Then I close my eyes and point to a word. I write that word down. I flip to another page and repeat this until I have six words. Then I try to write a story using all six of them. I may delete some of those words from a final version, but they have already forced me to think creatively.

When I studied children's poetry with Myra Cohn Livingston, our class did this multiword exercise. The resulting poems were so unique and powerful she put them into a collection titled *I'm Writing a Poem About … A Game of Poetry.*

The other assignment I give myself is to get a clean sheet of paper and choose an object to observe. It can be anything: a pencil, a scrap of cloth, an old ball, a penny, a snail, a leaf, a twig, a stamp. The possibilities are endless. Right now I'm going to observe my shoe. I write *Shoe* on the top of my paper. Then I divide my paper into four columns.

Over the first column, I write **facts**. Under this fact column, I write all the objective things I see and know about this shoe. For example I might list,

- black leather
- black laces
- comfortable fit
- good for walking
- inner arch support
- new clean soles
- highly polished
- smells new
- smooth leather
- bumpy laces

The heading of the second column is **fantasy.** Here I allow myself to go wild:

- What if my shoe were a pogo stick and everywhere I walked, I bounced?

- What if my shoe were magic and once I put it on, I could never take it off?

- What if my shoe were made of wax and melted whenever I went outside in summer?

- What if a mouse lived in my shoe?

The heading of my third column is **feelings**. These would be the feelings and memories my shoe brought to mind, like:

- The old X-ray machines that used to show us our foot bones and how well the shoe fit and now have been found to be extremely high in radiation danger.

- The first high-heeled shoes I wore hurt my feet so badly I had to take them off at the prom and dance in my stockings, which quickly shredded. A most embarrassing moment!

- The time I stepped on my boyfriend's toes and he let out a howl.

- The time I couldn't find my other everyday shoe and had to wear my shiny black party shoes to school.

- Those wonderful Mary Jane shoes that were for special occasions only.

- Dancing class in the fourth grade.

- The brown oxford shoes no one would ever wear today.

- My furry slippers shaped like a turtle.

- Turtle-shaped chocolate and nut candy.

The fourth column would be headed **fuzzy connections**. This is where I think in metaphor and simile.

- Black as night.
- Black as ink.

- Black as the bottom of a cruising ship.
- Black as tar, but not nearly so sticky.
- Snug as a muff.
- Shaped like a boat—all it needs is a sail.
- The laces are thin-ridged worms.
- Holes in the leather so the shoe can breathe? Is it alive?

Notice that many of my connections in this column, like *black as night* and *black as ink*, are tired and overused. But I wrote them down anyway. When filling in these columns, forget about editing. Now is the time for spilling guts, not for judgments. Note the crossover in the columns. Some observations, you might argue, belong in different columns. I don't worry about it. All I want to do is get everything down. The headings at the top of each column are there to get my creative juices in gear and moving. Once my mind starts traveling, I let it journey on.

When my mind is finally blank, I go back and think about possible writing ideas.

In my list, I like the idea of shoes that are pogo sticks. It's fun to imagine bouncing all around. Could I see into a bird's nest? Maybe I'll explore that.

Or I might write about those awful dance lessons and how humiliating it was not to be asked to dance.

Or maybe the mouse living in my shoe has something to say. These are two assignments I give myself when I am void of ideas. Usually I come up with something to write about.

Experiment with what gets your story juices flowing. If you've found an exercise from a book that works well for you, make that the seed you plant in your future.

## Your Writing Idea, or Tomato Seed, Was Underground and Finally Sprouted

What story ideas lurk inside your mind?

Often ideas stare at us, stomping up and down yelling, WRITE ME! But we don't see or hear them. Why not? Why is it so hard to write about the things that matter most to us?

Basically it's human nature, unless you're Donald Trump, to have self-doubt.

We don't find our own ideas interesting. They're such a part of our life they feel mundane.

We squash them before they get a chance to sprout because we don't believe others will care about them.

Here's a true story. In 1985 at an SCBWI conference, I attended a Saturday evening nonfiction talk. The speaker, Ross Olney, was tall, thin, and very imposing. He spoke with great self-assuredness, leaning over the podium and shaking his finger at the audience. "Write about what you know," he intoned.

Oh, that's easy for him, I thought. His life is full of exciting adventures. He races motorcycles. He skydives.

I slumped lower into my seat, feeling snail-small.

Probably most of you are like me and don't live dramatic lives. I've never saved anyone from drowning. I've never lived in a foreign country or hiked Mount Kilimanjaro. My parents never divorced. My husband and I recently celebrated our fortieth wedding anniversary. My children haven't spent any time in jail … yet!

Where was the drama in my life?

Who would buy a book, I wondered, about the shortest route between home and school, or how to make play dough, or stretch a pound of hamburger into dinner for six, or how to sew?

HOW TO SEW!

Just like in a cartoon, a lightbulb went on in my head.

Sewing!

I don't sew buttons. I don't sew hems or mend rips. I sew patchwork—quilts and pillows, dresses and toys, curtains and Christmas decorations. Once I even covered an entire room in tiny fabric squares. I couldn't wait to get home and start on *Eight Hands Round: A Patchwork Alphabet*.

Before that night in 1985, I thought the lack of drama in my life was a detriment. Now I accept and cherish my normal life and celebrate it as I write.

Do not, I beg you, discount your life as uninteresting to others. It's uninteresting to you because it is so familiar. To others it may be exotic. I am constantly bewildered when people rave about my patchwork and say how talented and artistic I am. I look at my quilts and can only see un-even stitches and pieces that don't fit at the corners. I know my quilts too well. To me my quilts are ordinary. To others they are extraordinary.

Trust that others will find beauty in your writing, too.

The acceptance that I have something to say from my own life was the single most important realization I've made as a writer. It turned me in the direction of writing stories that weren't second-rate imitations of other books in print, stories that did not get form rejections, and stories that would eventually be made into books.

How do you find what interests you?

You don't have to visit a therapist or delve into Freudian analysis. But you do need to spend time thinking about yourself, your past, your present, even your future.

One way is to keep a journal. It's not necessary to write in it every day. Write when inspiration hits you and about whatever you want. You can write about your activities, your dreams, your observations, your angers. Maybe you want to add newspaper clippings. Quotes or pictures might also find their way into your journal.

But the crucial thing is to go back periodically and read your journal. You'll find certain themes and subjects pop up frequently. Those are begging to be written. By *you!*

You say you don't want to keep a journal. Too time -onsuming? Too much of a commitment? Here's a shortcut.

Tap into your childhood memories by completing the following sentence fragments. Don't ponder your answers. Write the first things that come to your mind. Do not stop to edit. Write or type until you've exhausted each phrase and can't say anything more. Then go on to the next. Don't even think about completing the entire list. Do one at a time and when you come up with something that tugs at your heart, stop and write that story. The list will still be here for you whenever you need another writing prompt.

    a.  The first thing I ever remember was …

    b.  The things that made me mad as a child were …

    c.  I hated it when my mother …

    d.  I loved it when my mother …

e. I hated it when my father …

f. I loved it when my father …

g. I wish I'd learned how to …

h. My favorite foods as a child …

i. When I was a child I especially hated …

j. When I was a child more than anything I loved …

k. My best friend made me mad when …

l. It really bothered me when …

m. I was scared of …

n. The things I loved about growing up in the city/country/etc.

o. The things I hated about growing up in the city/country/etc.

p. At recess time, I loved …

q. At recess time, I hated …

r. The saddest thing that happened to me was …

s. The best things about winter were …

t. I hate winter because …

u. The fun things I did each summer were …

v. Each summer, I hated …

w. The best things about spring were …

x. The worst things about spring were …

y. The best things about fall …

z. How I hated each fall to …

aa. When I was young my parents made me …

bb. The most fun thing I did with my grandparents …

cc. My best memory of my siblings …

dd. It made me furious when my sibling …

ee. The most important adult in my life other than family … tell why …

ff. My favorite pet was … because …

gg. My favorite and least favorite games … because …

hh. The thing I worried about most when I was a child …

ii. The most embarrassing moment in my life …

jj. Sometimes I felt different because …

kk. What from my childhood would I like to do over again …

ll. My favorite books were …

mm. My favorite TV and movies when I was a child …

nn. The best thing that ever happened to me was …

oo. And anything else you'd like to share …

Perhaps you can think of other sentence fragments that might inspire you.

A story in my early-reader book *Silly Sadie, Silly Samuel* came out of my list. Filling it out reminded me how much I hated listening to my grandparents arguing. One would say the sky was blue. The other would say, "It's not really blue. I see a bit of gray there." I cringed while they bickered on and on and on. But years later, thanks to tapping into that memory, I was able to retell their arguing in a way that made children laugh.

Another thing you can do is think seriously about your interests, passions, and curiosities. Make a list of at least ten.

1. Things I love to do …
2. Things I'd like to do but haven't …
3. Things I want to know more about …
4. Things I enjoy reading about …

Notice that numbers 2 and 3 are not about things you have firsthand knowledge of, but of things you'd like to do and explore but haven't yet. My books *Mañana, Iguana, Fiesta Fiasco, Count on Culebra*, and *Tortuga in Trouble* were all inspired by my desire to learn Spanish. *Eight Hands Round: A Patchwork Alphabet* and *The Seasons Sewn: A Year in Patchwork*, as I've already mentioned, were inspired by my love of sewing quilts.

So now you have four ways to prime your pump and grow new stories. But everything depends on your being open to the new ideas that either come your way or that you cultivate.

Don't be a bud, closed and tight.

Be a blossom open to the sun, the wind, the rain, and any idea that comes your way.

## WHAT'S NEXT?

While you've been busy writing new stories, a publishing house was discussing your story ... favorably. In chapter 21 we'll look at what lies ahead.

## BEFORE YOU GO ON

1. Experiment with each of the ways to prime your own creative pump.

2. Choose an idea that grabs you.

3. Write that story.

4. Start all over again revising your story to publication.

5. Keep reading new picture books.

# CHAPTER 21

# SELLING YOUR MANUSCRIPT

*No writers ever forget their first acceptance. One fine day when I was seventeen I had my first, second, and third, all in the same morning's mail. Oh, I'm here to tell you, dizzy with excitement is no mere phrase.* —Truman Capote

If you're fortunate enough to sell your manuscript the first time out, or maybe many times out, celebrate. Call your husband, wife, partner, friends, children, and neighbors. Kiss the postal delivery person. Hug the clerk at the grocery checkout counter. Tell them all the fabulous news. Then treat yourself. Get a massage. Buy that watch you've had your eye on for months. Pop open champagne. You deserve it.

In case you're wondering, the joy of a sale never dissipates. I was as thrilled for my twentieth as I was for my first.

On the other hand, an editor may write saying she loves your manuscript but feels it needs work before she can offer a contract. Decision time! Do you agree with the suggestions offered? Then by all means go ahead and make the changes, knowing full well there's no guarantee of a contract.

But suppose you don't agree with the editorial suggestions. You think it will take your story to a place you weren't planning on visiting. Editors come in all different guises. Some are intelligent, astute, and understanding. Others are still learning those qualities. Some are fabulous about editing. Others are stronger at promoting and talking up your book.

If the editor's comments make you uncomfortable, trust your instincts and submit your story to another publisher *after* you have sent a letter to the first editor thanking her for her time and trouble with your manuscript. Indicate you will think about her suggestions. She doesn't have to know that you've already thought about them … negatively.

The reason to write is twofold. First of all, time will pass, and when you are not as close to your manuscript you might realize the editor is correct. On the other hand, you might still feel the same way, but at least you've made a friend in the business by thanking her for her effort.

Let's assume, for the purposes of this chapter, that the editor is contacting you with the best news possible.

## THE CONTRACT

When your feet have come back to earth, write down or ask the editor to e-mail, snail-mail, or fax the details. Tell her you're thrilled, but you'd like to look it over.

If you have an agent, he may have already negotiated the contract for you. If not, you need to study the offer and get advice from other published writers who are willing to share their experiences and even contracts. Organizations like The Authors Guild and SCBWI are both helpful. It would take an entire book and a law degree to go over the ins and outs of a contract. That's why I urge you to search for experts, or those who have had the experience before, to help you navigate the unfamiliar terms and complicated language.

## MORE REVISIONS

Unfortunately, even after the contract is signed and delivered, your work is not over yet. Unless you perfected the manuscript with your editor before you put your signature on that dotted line, you will need to do more revisions now. Some editors are hands-on and go through your manuscript with a fine eye. They may pick up big issues that need to be rethought. They may want you to strengthen the forward trajectory of your plot, revise the ending, or change the main character. They do this by sending you an editorial letter via snail mail or e-mail. Don't be surprised if this letter is longer than your manuscript.

Your manuscript will be included in the editorial letter along with lots of questions, corrections, and comments. When I showed my teen-age son Alan one story with all the editorial writings, he responded, "Mom, if I got a school paper back like that, I'd know I'd gotten a *D*."

Isn't it nice? In publishing we don't get graded.

Throughout this book I've emphasized how important it is to experiment with one's manuscript, to try different manners of telling, to come up with unique language, play around with openings, etc. You're exhausted from all your work up to this point. How can there be more?

Easy! Your editor is another fresh eye to your story. She brings with her a publishing and marketing background that you probably haven't tapped into yet. Be grateful! Consider this time with your editor as another opportunity to revisit, revise, and improve.

Of course, there will be times when the two of you disagree. If the issue is important for you, state calmly and clearly why you want to keep the writing as it is. When faced with a reasonable explanation, editors will usually defer to you, as they should. After all, your name goes on the cover, and you are the one who will feel the brunt of reviews.

Be reasonable, however. Don't let your hair stand on end at every comment. Don't slam down the phone or stop talking. That wouldn't be the way to resolve issues in a marriage, and it won't work here. Honesty, stated graciously, is always the best policy. Notice the words *stated graciously*. You want your editor to buy future manuscripts. Keep the relationship calm and happy.

After you are done working with the editor, the copy editor will have his turn with your manuscript. He should be a whiz at grammar and punctuation. He might even be rigid about these issues and suggest changes that are in opposition to the music of your text. Everything is negotiable as long as you can make your points calmly and professionally.

After the copyediting, your words only will be printed in the font style and size of the future book. You will be given one last look. This is when I go into anxiety attack mode. Help! My story is really, truly going to be published, exposed to all the world (and I have to make sure it's right. I'm like Konrad Lorenz, who said, "During the final stages of publishing a paper or book, I always feel strongly repelled by my own writing ... it appears increasingly hackneyed and banal and less worth publishing."

Let those self-criticisms wash over you like a spring shower. This is fear and self-loathing talking. What you have written is fine. Your group agrees. You editor agrees. So does the publishing house. They wouldn't have bought it if they didn't.

Your job as a professional is to go over the text and make sure every *I* is dotted and every *T* is crossed. Sue Alexander used to read her manuscripts backwards to ensure the careful attention required to pick up errors on a text she knew too well. I've never done that, but I do read mine out loud several—okay many—times. Major changes at this stage may cost money, but if you're convinced of that necessity, go for it.

As the years have gone by and the number of my published books increased, I recognize the panic I feel at this stage and work hard to alleviate my reactions by spending as much concentrated time as I need on earlier editorial revisions.

# CHOOSING AN ILLUSTRATOR

Alas, that is not your job. The editor is the one who, often in consultation with the art director and others, has that responsibility. He probably will not even consult you about it. In fact, the illustrator may have been chosen before you were even offered a contract.

Now that I'm well published, editors occasionally ask me if I have strong feelings about an illustrator, or maybe even have a suggestion of one for them. Their question, however, is always qualified with "I can't guarantee that I'll pay any attention to you."

When you first hear the name of your illustrator, you'll probably rush to your local bookstore or library or check online to see his work.

Maybe you'll be thrilled. Maybe you'll be disappointed. Most likely, you'll need time to adapt to the artist's style.

This concept of handing one's manuscript over to an artist not of one's choosing may be difficult. It calls for a huge amount of trust on your part.

Let me ease your mind. Although I know writers who have been disappointed in the art for their books, my experience has been the exact opposite, even when an editor has named an illustrator whose image at first appears diametrically opposed to mine.

Life and books both have a way of working out for the best. In one case of mine, the editor was correct in her selection and the book turned out better than I would have imagined. Another time the editor finally saw the same light I had seen and removed the artist from the project.

Illustrators are chosen for a myriad of reasons unknown to the writer. Perhaps the illustrator has a famous name and the publishing house hopes that will translate to strong sales. Although you may be distressed by the artist's style in previous books, he may be eager to try a new approach, and your story offers him that opportunity. Perhaps the editor wants to go against expectation with your story. Her first choice of an artist may be booked up through 2020. Maybe the publishing house is afraid an up-and-coming artist might start working with another house if she doesn't get a new project soon. Whatever the cause, the end result is the same. You have an illustrator. Congratulations!

Will you get to see the evolution of the artist's thinking about your story, i.e., a dummy, sample art, finished art? The answer varies from house to house. Some editors make sure that I have a chance to see and comment on the work. Other editors keep it a closely guarded secret.

Why would they do that?

Let me tell you another story. An artist friend of mine received a manuscript about a child's relationship with her two grandfathers. She sent in her rough sketches and the editor, this time being very generous, showed them to the writer, who was immediately upset because the grandfathers in the sketches didn't look at all like her grandfathers. She even offered to share photos with the illustrator. NO! NO! NO! Imagine if an illustrator told us how to write our story. It's not (unless they do both) their expertise. In the same way, we can't tell them how to illustrate our book.

Picture books are collaborations. Just as we writers struggle to tell our story the best possible way, artists do, too. They are expected to bring their unique personality, style, and talent to each new project. Telling my friend how her grandfathers should look is as inappropriate as insisting your child go to law school when his dream is to be a pop singer. Wise parents permit children to follow their dreams (assuming they can support themselves). Let your illustrator follow hers.

If your manuscript is nonfiction or a historical story, you can rightfully request to see the illustrations to verify the art reflects the truth. Often in these circumstances, the illustrator might even contact you, through the editor, to ask for some research guidance.

# WAITING FOR PUBLICATION

The time from the wonderful call, e-mail, or however your editor approached you with the happy news of a sale to the time your book is published can take as much, or more, time as an elephant's twenty-two-month pregnancy. Most of my books took two years and one book, five!

What are you to do during that period? Certainly not sit around and wait! You need to start a new story, which we covered in chapter 20.

And in between work at your computer, use the time to get a heads-up in promoting your book. Chances are excellent that your book will not be the only one your publisher produces that season. They will be pushing your book along with all the others on their list. So here are some things you might consider doing:

**1. Update your mailing list.** Perhaps you will want to send a snail-mail or e-mail announcement about your book. Don't be shy. I suspect few people would consider me pushy or aggressive, but I've come to feel that, just as I like to hear about friends' good news, they probably want to hear about mine. And if they don't, they can just drop my letter in the recycle bin or press the delete button. No harm done.

**2. Make a list of newspapers** that might be interested in a story about your book.

Introduce yourself to booksellers. If you'd like to do a signing or presentation when the book comes out, tell them. They will be more apt to do such an event if you can provide a list of people living locally for them to contact.

**3. Get to know your librarian** (if you don't already). Attend their story hours. Offer to give one.

The marketing people will no doubt have you complete a questionnaire about possible important contacts and to inquire about what you are willing to do in support of your book. Be honest. If you can't speak to an auditorium of squirming kindergarteners, say so.

Promotion requires new skills for writers. Many of us are drawn to this work because we prefer to be alone, to mull over issues and share our view of the world hidden behind the covers of a book.

Now, however, you must start practicing your people and performance skills. Sometime in your career you'll be invited to give a talk to children and a wide range of adults—teachers, librarians, and other writers. You may be terrified about speaking and prefer taking out the trash or eating a plate full of liver (both of which I hate!) to standing in front of strangers.

During this lag time before publication, work on improving your comfort level for these appearances. Take an acting or a public speaking class. Deliver a talk to your mirror. Don't neglect your writing, however. I once heard a bookstore owner say that the best promotion was to publish a new book.

## THE BIG DAY—PUBLICATION

Here at last! The day you've been dreaming about. You've received the catalog announcing your book and gotten your author's copies. Maybe you've even read some reviews.

Wonderful reviews! Not so wonderful reviews! Maybe a horrible review! You won't be alone. We all get them at one time or another in our careers. And they can be devastating to your ego, but please slip them into a faraway drawer and go on with your business.

The amazing thing about reviews is their wide variety. One early reader of mine, *Silly Sadie, Silly Samuel*, received the most fantastic reviews of my career. I was sure it would be a winner. Then it received a terrible review from *School Library Journal*. An early reader obviously needs the school and library market, so the book died quietly.

The easiest way to deal with reviews, good or bad, is not to pay attention to them. Going into a funk for days or weeks is a huge waste of time and emotional energy. You can't change the world by complaining or withdrawing, but you can write another story.

Let's return to the publication date—that magic moment when booksellers will finally have your baby in hand. While you may anticipate the day, I'm sorry to disillusion you: the world probably won't. In fact, it will most likely come and go unnoticed by everyone but your immediate family and close friends.

When I was young and my beloved grandfather died, I was furious that the world didn't stop to recognize its loss and my pain. Eventually I understood that *my* world may have been forever changed, but the *whole* world didn't even know my grandfather or my sadness. His death prepared me for what was to come in my career. While I still have niggling hopes that firecrackers might go off and TV reporters knock on my door, I'm more realistic. I don't let that newly acquired insight stop me from enjoying my proud moment. You shouldn't, either. Be like James M. Barrie, who said, "For several days after my first book was published I carried it about in my pocket, and took surreptitious peeps at it to make sure the ink had not faded."

Carry your book around, read it over and over, and then go back to your computer. Start writing another wonderful book.

## WHAT'S NEXT?

Nothing ... except for an epilogue, acknowledgments, a bibliography, copyright information, and index. You already know how to write, revise, and submit your picture book manuscript. Now it's up to you.

# EPILOGUE

 *All good writing is swimming under*
*water and holding your breath.*
—*F. Scott Fitzgerald*

If you've taken your time reading this book and doing the exercises, you've discovered writing picture books is not as easy as you had imagined. While I'm from the school of "the more effort one puts in the more satisfying the outcome," you may worry if every story is going to require the same kind of attention to detail.

Clyde Bulla wrote this note to me several years ago on a Christmas card:

> Sometimes when I look back on the seventy odd (books) published under my name I think someone else must have written them. If I did write them, why haven't I learned something from the writing? Why does each book seem to pose a new set of problems? And what's with beginning? Why is each one so nearly impossible?

So if you ask me if you're going to have to struggle through each story you write, I would have to answer "yes and no."

*Yes* because no two stories will be the same. Every new writing project will create problems, some big, some little, some you've faced before and others that might throw you for a loop. Each story requires expanding your creative approaches to solving those problems. It's an exciting, challenging process.

But the answer is also *no* because the more you write, the more you pay attention to the subjects covered in this book, the more you

read in the field, the more knowledge you will acquire for the next story. Because I've been doing this so long, I rarely color highlight my openings anymore. The six *W*s have become so ingrained in my mind, I don't need to anymore. But I still make sure those six *W*s are all right up in the front of my story.

The same thing will happen to you. The more you write and the more you do these exercises, the more they will become second nature to you.

Writing will never be easy. Struggle is part of the game. However, if you're feeling down and discouraged and looking for a reason to keep going, I'd like to close with this story.

Years ago, my surgeon husband and I went out to dinner with another physician and his wife. We didn't know them well but thought we might have something in common.

The evening was a disaster.

This doctor (I'll call him Dr. Full-of-Himself) kept trying to impress upon me what important work he and my husband did.

Don't get me wrong. I believe my husband's work is incredibly vital, especially to his patients. But Dr. Full-of-Himself would not give up. Conversation throughout the evening centered on medicine and how wonderful and important doctors are. At one point, his voice grew low and serious. He stared directly into my eyes. "Think about it," he said, cupping his hands in front of me. "Every day, your husband holds life in his hands."

It was all I could do to not cough my food into his face. Talk about self-importance! That phrase of holding life in his hands has become a standing joke in our house whenever my husband starts acting too cocky or self-important.

But it got me thinking about what you and I do.

We picture book writers don't hold children's lives in our hands. Thank goodness! I couldn't stand the stress.

However, we introduce children to the pleasures of reading. If we give them good stories, they will remember reading with fondness. They will want to go on and read early readers and then chapter books and middle-grade novels and YA novels and adult novels, textbooks, newspapers, computer screens, and magazines.

We are the first step up the ladder to create lifetime readers.

Without a thoughtful, educated, and well-read population, how can we solve the many problems—environment, health care, schools, wars—facing us? We picture book writers hold something important in our hands. We hold the world's future.

So keep going. Keep struggling. Keep revising and writing. Walter de la Mare said, "Only the rarest kind of best in anything can be good enough for the young." That best must be our goal with each story we write.

You're on your own now, but fear not. This book is always available for your reference.

I wish you not only happy writing, but challenging writing and the publication of memorable books for children ... stories that will inspire them to read more and more and more. You can do it!

# ACKNOWLEDGMENTS

 *"My friends are my estate."*
—Emily Dickenson

Although I wrote this book alone in my office, many people in spirit hovered over my shoulder to make sure I got it right. They prodded me on, reminded me of lessons learned, and shared their expertise.

Linda Zuckerman, my former editor, now special friend, has invited me back to Portland to speak each July at the Pacific Northwest Children's Book Conference (www.ceed.pdx.edu/children). Many of the talks I gave there have been adapted into this book.

Over thirty years ago I discovered UCLA Extension Writers' Program, and it was a timid, doubtful young mother who first walked into a class taught by Sonia Levitin. Without her encouragement, I would never have signed up for future classes with her and other fine teachers Sue Alexander and Myra Cohn Livingston. Sue and Myra, both from the school of tough love, never held back in their criticisms. While I often found their comments painful, I appreciated that they never stopped prodding me to do my best. I can't thank them enough.

UCLA Extension Writers' Program also gave me the first opportunity to teach about my passion, and I thank them (especially Linda Venis) for trusting a novice. In addition, I'm grateful to my students, whose questions and works-in-progress inspired some of these exercises and forced me to articulate my writing process. More gratitude than she will ever know goes to former student Molly Nickell, who suggested I should write this book.

The Society of Children's Book Writers & Illustrators' publications, conferences, and advice have helped make me the published writer I am today. Many speakers I've heard at their workshops have shared wisdom and exercises that has crept into this book.

Over the years I've learned much from my editors. It's always surprising how a story I'd thought ready for publication still needed work. I thank Mary

Cash, Nora Cohen, Dianne Hess, Ruth Katcher, Melanie Kroupa, Kevin Lewis, and Linda Zuckerman for making each of my books better than I could have imagined. Special recognition must go to my editor Alice Pope. The jump from 350-word manuscripts to 250 pages was terrifying, but Alice was patient, helpful, and encouraging.

Writing would be a lonely task without fabulously talented writers in my critique groups. In Los Angeles I work with Erica Silverman and Karen Winnick. We are forever grateful to Sue Alexander for bringing us together and sharing her knowledge with us. She is much missed. Evolving from a ten-day workshop, Centrum Port Townsend Writers' Conference (www.centrum.org) with Jane Yolen, my other group's members live all across the United States. We call ourselves *The Write Sisters*. Tricia Gardella, Helen Ketteman, Kirby Larson, Mary Nethery, Dian Curtis Regan, and Vivian Sathre try to meet in person at least once a year and critique via e-mail in the time between.

Another group, PJ Lutz, Brian Rocklin, Rebecca Delfino, Armineh Manookian, Cindy Moussas-Holmes, and Sheri Linden, worked with me specifically on the proposal for this book. Others who read a part, or all, of the manuscript are Sue Alexanber, Karen Winnick, Erica Silverman, Mary Nethery, and Kirby Larson.

Thanks to all my other writing buddies who over the years have shared their talent and wisdom. I've learned so much from you. I could not begin to list all the librarians and bookstore owners who have supported my career, tracked down hard-to-find references, and introduced me to new and exciting books. Special thanks though must go to Diane Applebaum at Children's Book World in Los Angeles (www.childrensbookworld.com) who, no matter what question I brought regarding examples for this book, had the answer at her fingertips.

My interest in picture books would never have been born without my four children, Henya, Jon, Alan, and Sarah. Our bedtime readings inspired me to write. Now my grandchildren, Hazel and Lena, listen to my stories and say and do things that spark new story ideas.

My father instilled in me a love of quotes. He is no longer living but would have been pleased at my opening each chapter with a quotation. At the young age of ninety-three, my mother, Genevieve Smith Whitford, a poet and former humor magazine editor, read this manuscript from beginning to end. I'm grateful for her fine suggestions.

The biggest thanks of all go to my husband, Ron, who every evening insists on washing the dishes because "You have important work to do." I would still be unpublished were it not for his understanding, support, and love.

# INDEX